The Schlumpf Automobile Collection

Tri-lingual edition

A documentation by Wolfgang Drehsen, Werner Haas and Hans-Jürgen Schneider, edited by Halwart Schrader.

Schiffer Publishing Ltd

West Chester, Pennsylvania 19380

D1091845

Published by Schiffer Publishing, Ltd.
1469 Morstein Road
West Chester, Pennsylania 19380
Please write for a free catalog
This book may be purchased from the publisher.
Please include $2.00 postage.
Try your bookstore first.

Tri-lingual edition

Die Automobile der Gebrüder Schlumpf

Eine Dokumentation von
Wolfgang Drehsen, Werner Haas und
Hans-Jürgen Schneider
Herausgegeben von Halwart Schrader

Les voitures des frères Schlumpf

Une documentation rassemblée par
Wolfgang Drehsen, Werner Haas et
Hans-Jürgen Schneider, et présentée
par Halwart Schrader.

The Schlumpf Automobile Collection

A documentation by Wolfgang Drehsen,
Werner Haas and Hans-Jürgen
Schneider, edited by Halwart Schrader.

Alle Fahrzeuge waren sorgfältig abgedeckt, ehe die Fotos
zu diesem Buch gemacht
wurden.

Toutes les voitures étaient bien
protégées. Le photographe a
dû commencer par retirer les
feuilles et toiles de protection...

Before our photographers could
start working, every car had to
be unwrapped most carefully.

Inhalt
Index
Contents

Zum Verständnis dieses Buches.

In aller Bescheidenheit darf dieses Buch für sich in Anspruch nehmen, als einmalig zu gelten. Es enthält Fotos von allen Exponaten der größten, wertvollsten und für lange Zeit geheimsten Automobilsammlung Europas. An Stückzahlen – kaum an Wert – wird sie nur noch von der voluminösen Kollektion William Harrahs in Reno, Nevada, übertroffen.

Harrahs Sammlung indessen läßt System erkennen. Er hat konsequent Amerikaner zusammentragen, oft lückenlose Fabrikationsprogramme. Einige Europäer sind seine highlights. Aber es scheint Harrah nicht in erster Linie um Kostbarkeiten zu gehen. Im Gegensatz zu den Sammlern Schlumpf.

Dieses Buch ist aber weitaus mehr als ein Katalog wertvoller Automobile. Es ist der Beweis einer journalistischen Glanzleistung, die der Kölner Fotograf Wolfgang Drehsen und seine Pressekollegen Werner Haas und Hans-Jürgen Schneider vollbrachten, als sie unter den widrigsten Umständen diese 470 Fotos (und es waren noch einige mehr) anfertigten. Zu einem Zeitpunkt, als nach turbulenten Tagen voller extremer Beschlüsse und Gegenbeschlüsse aller von der Affäre Schlumpf betroffenen Personen und Institutionen das Museum für die Öffentlichkeit schon fast wieder ‚tabu' war, gelang es ihnen, in einem Tag-und-Nacht-Marathon Hunderte von Filmen zu belichten. Aber es wurde nicht nur fotografiert – mindestens ebenso viel Fleiß verwendete das Team auf das sorgfältige Abdecken der vielen mit Papierbahnen und Tüchern verhängten Fahrzeuge, das äußerst behutsame und von den

Afin de mieux comprendre ce livre.

Toute modestie gardée, cet ouvrage peut affirmer son caractère exceptionnel. Il contient des photos de tous les objets de la plus grande, de la plus précieuse collection automobile en Europe, de celle aussi qui fut longtemps la plus secrète. Seule l'énorme collection de William Harrah, à Reno dans le Névada la dépasse; par le nombre, par la valeur à peine.

La collection Harrah laisse reconnaître un certain ordre. Son propriétaire s'intéresse avant tout aux productions américaines, et il essaye de reconstituer des séries où chaque modèle est représenté par un seul exemplaire. Les Schlumpf en revanche rassemblèrent tout ce qui leur semblait précieux, et acquirent souvent deux ou trois exemplaires du même modèle.

Cet ouvrage est beaucoup plus qu'un simple catalogue d'automobiles prestigieuses. Il est aussi le témoin d'une prouesse journalistique accomplie par le photographe Wolfgang Drehsen, de Cologne, ainsi que par ses collègues Werner Haas et Hans-Jürgen Schneider. En effet, dans des conditions extrêmement difficiles ils ont réalisé les 470 photos que nous vous présentons (et quelques autres encore!) Après ces journées mouvementées où tous ceux concernés par l'affaire Schlumpf, gens et institutions, s'enfermaient à l'extrême dans un jeu de décisions et de contre-décisions, à un moment où le musée à nouveau était devenu «tabou», les trois hommes, travaillant jour et nuit, ont réussi dans une course folle à réaliser des centaines de pellicules. Mais ils n'ont pas simplement photographié – il leur a fallu en vérité mettre autant de

For a better appreciation of this book

The claim that this is a unique publication is not an immodest one. It contains photos of all the objects in the largest, most valuable and – until very recently – best hidden automobile collection in Europe. Indeed, it is a collection that is exceeded in numbers, though hardly in value, by the giant assemblage of William Harrah in Reno, Nevada.

William Harrah's collection can easily be differentiated from the Schlumpf's. The Reno museum presents a more or less complete cross-section of the American automobile industry (some European high-lights included), while in Mulhouse almost everything is on display Fritz Schlumpf could get hold of. Type 46 and 57 Bugattis by the dozen may add immense value to the collection; but this mass demonstration does neither disclose the French motor car's evolution in general nor in particular. It reveals a mania for a marque.

This book, however, is far more than a catalog of valuable automobiles. It is the printed evidence of a brilliant journalistic performance by the Cologne photographer Wolfgang Drehsen and his editorial colleagues Werner Haas and Hans-Jürgen Schneider, who produced these 470 photographs (and there were even more) under the most adverse conditions. At a time when, after many turbulent days of decisions and counter-decisions by people and institutions affected by the Schlumpf Affair, the museum had again become „off limits", they were able to expose hundreds of rolls of film in a day-and-night-marathon. But this was not just a photography session. At least as much effort went into uncovering the cars, which were

Wolfgang Drehsen (linkes Bild) mit seinem Kollegen Schneider und dem Schweizer Journalisten Lienhard (rechtes Bild).

Le photographe Wolfgang Drehsen (à gauche) et son collègue Schneider et le journaliste Suisse Lienhard (à droite).

Photographer Wolfgang Drehsen (left) and his team mate Schneider and the Swiss journaliste Lienhard (right).

strengen Argusaugen der Begleiter vom Betriebsrat überwachte Entfernen der Staubschichten auf dem (meist) makellosen Lack, das Ausmessen und -rechnen der Beleuchtungsverhältnisse. Denn es verstand sich von selbst, daß Wolfgang Drehsen nicht mit großem Ateliergepäck in die Schlumpf'schen Hallen ziehen konnte. Wer einmal in geschlossenen Räumen, ausschließlich bei Misch- oder Kunstlicht, in gedrängten Platzverhältnissen Automobile fotografierte und um die Probleme störender Reflexe, zu dicht stehender Nachbarwagen, unruhiger Hintergründe und zur Eile gemahnender Aufseher weiß, kann ermessen, welche Arbeit in diesem Buch steckt. Sicher haben Sie auch Verständnis dafür, wenn bei einigen Fahrzeugen die Schutzhüllen nicht ganz fallen konnten oder andere - kosmetische - Details den Genuß am perfekten Bild beeinträchtigen. Die letzten Fotos entstanden im Rückwärtsgang, als die Journalisten letztendlich - höflich, aber bestimmt - aus dem Saal komplimentiert wurden ...

Es sei an dieser Stelle klargestellt, daß die Bilder dieses Buches nicht illegal zustande kamen. Sie wurden mit der ausdrücklichen Genehmigung der Gewerkschaftsleitung aufgenommen, die zum damaligen Zeitpunkt für das Museum die Verantwortung innehatte.

In diesem Zusammenhang sei auch darauf hingewiesen, daß die *Auto Zeitung*, der Drehsen, Haas und Schneider als Profis schon seit langem angehören, (ihre sorgfältig recherchierten Berichte sind branchenbekannt) als erste Publi-

soin à retirer les nombreuses feuilles et toiles de protection qui recouvraient les véhicules; à enlever avec mille précautions et sous le regard sévère et attentif des membres accompagnateurs du comité d'entreprise les couches de poussière qui cachaient une peinture le plus souvent impeccable; à mesurer et à calculer afin de tirer le meilleur parti possible de l'éclairage. Car on comprendra aisément que Wolfgang Drehsen n'a pas pu entrer dans les halls de la maison Schlumpf avec un important matériel. Celui qui a déjà photographié des voitures en intérieur, uniquement à la lumière artificielle ou avec un éclairage mixte, sans avoir le recul souhaitable, celui qui connaît le problème des reflets gênants, des véhicules tassés les uns contre les autres, des arrière-plans mouvants, des gardiens qui toujours vous pressent, celui-là seulement pourra mesurer tout le travail que représente ce livre. C'est pourquoi on sera sans doute indulgent si pour quelques véhicules les bâches de protection n'ont pu tomber totalement, ou si certains détails d'aspect empêchent de savourer pleinement une photo parfaite. Les dernières prises de vues ont été réalisées à reculons, lorsque finalement - de manière polie mais ferme - on a raccompagné nos journalistes vers la sortie.

Il faut noter que toutes les photos de cette publication ont été réalisées de manière officielle et non pas illégale. La direction syndicale qui détenait à l'époque la responsabilité totale de la collection Schlumpf, a donné son accord exprès pour que soient prises les photos.

decked with cloth and paper and at all times watched over by Argus-eyed members of the shop council; into the extremely careful dusting-off of mostly immaculate paint; into the painstaking measurement and interpretation of the lighting conditions.

It goes pretty well without saying that Wolfgang Drehsen was not allowed to move into the Halls of Schlumpf with a full complement of studio equipment. And anyone who has had to photograph automobiles in artificial light, who has had to deal with the perplexities of disturbing reflections, cars too close to each other, cluttered backgrounds and the „hurry along, please" of a museum supervisor, can imagine the work that went into this book. The reader will understand, then, when a few vehicles appear still partially covered, or when cosmetic details may not be quite perfect. The last few photos were taken in reverse gear, as the journalists were finally accompanied, politely but firmly, out of the hall ...

I would like to point out, by the way, that all photographs shown on the following pages have been taken by official permission. Our team was authorized to enter the museum by CFDT officials who were in charge for the responsibility for the museum.

In this connection it should be mentioned that *Auto Zeitung* was the first publication in its field to report details about the Schlumpf Affair and print photos that had never before been revealed - in early December 1976. That report was not in the nature of a front-page sensation, but rather an account of

8

kation der gesamten Automobilwelt Europas schon Anfang Dezember 1976 Einzelheiten zu den Hintergründen der Affäre Schlumpf brachte und bislang nie veröffentlichte Fotos zeigen konnte. Dabei ging es nicht um eine vordergründige Sensation, sondern um die sachliche Darlegung von Fakten, die vor allem in französischen Wirtschaftskreisen schon einige Zeit Gegenstand bislang unbestätigter Gerüchte waren. Daß die recht delikate Affäre Schlumpf zu einem Thema geriet, an welchem keines der mehr oder weniger renommierten Automobil- und Publikums-Journale im Verlauf des ersten Halbjahres 1977 vorbeikam, rechtfertigt die Entscheidung, diese Dokumentation herauszugeben, einmal mehr.

Halwart Schrader

Nous aimerions rappeler ici que c'est *Auto Zeitung* qui a été la première publication spécialisée à révéler dès le début de décembre 1976 des détails sur les dessous de l'affaire Schlumpf et qui a fait paraître des photos que personne ne connaissait jusqu'alors. Il ne s'agissait pas d'une nouvelle à sensation, mais d'un exposé objectif de faits qui avaient donné lieu depuis quelque temps à certaines rumeurs, en particulier dans les milieux d'affaires français, des rumeurs que personne ne confirmait. La très délicate affaire Schlumpf est devenue un sujet qu'aucune publication automobile ou générale, connue ou moins connue, n'a pu éviter dans les six premiers mois de l'année 1977, et cela justifie une nouvelle fois notre décision de faire paraître cet ouvrage.

Halwart Schrader

facts that had already long been rumored in French business circles. The fact that this delicate affair turned into a topic that none of the more-or-less respected auto and general publications could ignore in the first half of 1977, justifies our decision to publish this book all the more.

Halwart Schrader

Hintergründe der Affäre Schlumpf.

Alle Automobil-Liebhaber und -Sammler hatten auf diesen Augenblick gewartet: Auf die Möglichkeit, die geheimnisvolle Kollektion einmaliger Fahrzeuge aus neun Jahrzehnten zu besichtigen, zusammengetragen von zwei Brüdern aus der elsässischen Textildynastie. Niemand glaubte daran, daß dieser Wunsch jemals in Erfüllung gehen würde. Bis im Sommer 1976 in Malmerspach eine Zeitbombe zu ticken begann, die am 6. Oktober eine erste Explosion auslöste.

Fritz Schlumpf, Jahrgang 1906, und sein Bruder Hans, Jahrgang 1904, die Textilkönige des Elsaß, konnten den Triumph ihres Lebens nicht mehr auskosten. Die pompöse Eröffnung des ‚Monument Bugatti' wurde durch ein überfallartiges Spektakulum ersetzt, als offenbar wurde, daß die Kammgarn-spinnerei Malmerspach im Thann-Tal sowie die Firma Gluck & Cie. bankrott waren. Die Oldtimer-Leidenschaft der Brüder Schlumpf hatte nicht allein einen Verlust von 1800 Arbeitsplätzen gekostet, sondern auch den Traum zunichte gemacht, in Mülhausen die wertvollste Automobilsammlung der Welt als eine anerkannte Gedenkstätte der Automobilindustrie Frankreichs, wenn nicht Europas, zu etablieren. Die mit allen erdenklichen Sicherheitsvor-kehrungen geschützte Schlumpf-Kollek-tion, die im Laufe der Jahre kaum mehr als zwei Dutzend Auserwählte sehen durften, wurde über Nacht dem Publikum zugänglich gemacht, wenn auch aus ganz anderen Beweggründen, als es die Schlumpf-Brüder wohl je im Sinn hatten. Es dürften etwa 50 000 Menschen gewesen sein, die in

Les dessous de l'affaire Schlumpf.

Tous les amateurs d'automobiles et tous les collectionneurs avaient attendu cet instant, avaient espéré pouvoir visiter la mystérieuse collection de véhicules uniques construits durant une période de quatre-vingt-dix ans et rassemblés par deux frères appartenant à une dynastie du textile alsacien. Personne ne croyait vraiment que ce voeu serait un jour exaucé, jusqu'à l'été 1976, lorsque à Malmerspach une bombe à retardement se mit à produire son tic-tac pour amener une première détonation le 6 octobre.

Fritz Schlumpf, né en 1906, et son frère Hans, né en 1904, deux rois du textile en Alsace, se retrouvaient dans l'impossibilité de goûter le triomphe de leur vie. Lorsqu'il fut patent que la filature de Malmerspach dans la vallée de la Thur et la firme Gluck et Cie étaient en faillite, le faste prévu pour l'inauguration du Monument Bugatti fut remplacé par une action qui avait le caractère d'un coup de main. La

The Backgrounds of the Schlumpf Affair.

Every automobile enthusiast and collector had waited for this moment – the moment when the secret collection of unique vehicles from nine decades, assembled by two brothers of the Alsatian textile dynasty, would finally become accessible. Nobody really believed anymore that the moment would come ... until a time bomb began to tick in Malmerspach in the summer of 1976. On October 6 it set off the first explosion.

Fritz Schlumpf, born in 1906, and his two-year-older brother Hans would no longer be able to enjoy the triumph of their lives. The pompous opening ceremony of the "Bugatti Monument" was to be replaced by a hardly propitious spectacle when it became known that Malmerspach Spinnery in the Thann Valley, as well as the firm Gluck & Cie., had gone bankrupt. As it would turn out, the Schlumpf brothers' enthusiasm for vintage automobiles had not only cost

Fritz Schlumpf, 1967

Diese Bilder sollten nach dem Willen der Schlumpfs nicht noch einmal erscheinen. Im Mai 1965 wurden sie anläßlich eines Besuches illustrer Gäste gemacht.

Les Schlumpf ne voulaient pas que ces photos paraissent une deuxième fois. Elles ont été prises en mai 1965 à l'occasion de la visite d'invités de marque.

The Schlumpfs did not want these pictures to ever appear again. They were taken on the occasion of the visit of a group of illustrous guests.

Rekordzeit durch die Hallen eilten. Fotoreporter aus aller Welt drückten hastig und ziemlich wahllos auf die Auslöser ihrer Kameras, Autonostalgiker hakten ihre Listen ab. Die ersten Kühlerfiguren verschwanden. Derweil saßen Hans und Fritz Schlumpf in ihrer Suite des Hotels ‚Des Trois Rois' zu Basel, wohl mit dem Schicksal hadernd, das ihnen keine Chance mehr zugestehen wollte.

Fangen wir die Geschichte von vorne an. Fritz und Hans Schlumpf wuchsen als Sprößlinge eines Schweizer Textilkaufmannes in Omegna in der Nähe Mailands auf – in der gleichen Gegend wie ihr später vergöttertes Idol Ettore Bugatti. 1919, nach dem Tode des Vaters, zog die Familie wieder in die Heimat der Mutter, nach Mülhausen im Elsaß. Auch Bugatti war, wenn auch mit einigen Umwegen, von Mailand nach dem Elsaß gezogen …

Hans Schlumpf begann eine Banklehre, Fritz ging in ein Maklerbüro. In der Weltwirtschaftskrise zu Anfang der dreißiger Jahre bewies er das erste Mal, daß er ein geschickter Kaufmann war.

passion des frères Schlumpf pour les voitures anciennes n'avait pas seulement provoqué la disparition de 1800 emplois, elle avait aussi réduit à néant le rêve d'établir à Mulhouse la collection automobile la plus prestigieuse du monde. La collection Schlumpf, qui bénéficiait de tous les systèmes de protection qu'on peut imaginer, et que deux douzaines de personnes tout au plus ont pu admirer au cours des ans, s'est du jour au lendemain ouverte au public, il est vrai toutefois que c'était pour des raisons tout autres que ce qu'avaient jamais pu concevoir les deux frères. On peut estimer à environ 50 000 le nombre de personnes qui en un temps record se pressèrent dans les halls qui leur

1800 jobs but shattered the dream of establishing the world's most valuable car collection in Mulhouse, officially, at least.

The Schlumpf Collection, protected by every imaginable security measure and seen by no more than two dozen chosen human beings over the years, was opened to the public overnight – but for totally different reasons than anything the Schlumpfs hat in mind. Now, in record time, something like 50,000 people had hurried through these halls, which surely seemed like a treasury to them. Photographers from all over the world made their way through the collection, tripping their shutters at random; nostalgic auto fans checked off their lists. The first radiator ornaments disappeared. And during all this, Hans and Fritz Schlumpf sat in their suite in the Hotel des Trois Rois in Basel, quite probably trying to come to terms with the reality that they have no chance of recovering their treasures.

But let us begin at the beginning. Fritz and Hans Schlumpf, offspring of a Swiss textile merchant, grew up in

Ein geheimes Foto, das 1966 dennoch an die Öffentlichkeit gelangte: der 16-Zylinder Bugatti Typ 45, von dem es nur zwei Stück gab.

Une photo secrète qui pourtant fut rendue publique en 1966: Bugatti du type 45, 16 cylindres qui n'a été construite qu'en deux exemplaires.

A secret photo that nevertheless found its way into the press: the 16-cylinder Bugatti 45, of which only two examples were built.

Diese Fabrikhalle beherbergt die kostbare Schlumpf-Sammlung. Ein immenser Gebäudekomplex!

Ce hall d'usine abrite la précieuse collection Schlumpf. Un énorme complexe architectural... This factory houses the invaluable Schlumpf collection – an immense hall.

Einer seiner engen Mitarbeiter erinnerte sich: „Fritz Schlumpf galt als fabelhafter Spekulierer. Er stieg unaufhaltsam zur Finanzelite Frankreichs auf." Hans und Fritz investierten ihr Geld in Aktien und erwarben 1938 die alte Kammgarnspinnerei in Malmerspach. Sie profitierten von dem Umstand, daß die jüdischen Eigentümer – wie man heute in Malmerspach sagt – infolge nationalsozialistischen Drucks, der auch im Elsaß zu spüren war, ihre Anlagen alsbald verkaufen mußten und auswanderten. Dann brach der Krieg aus. Eine große Reihe von Verdiensten sagt man den Brüdern Schlumpf nach, wenn die Rede auf soziale Einrichtungen für die Arbeiter kommt – doch das liegt natürlich bereits Jahrzehnte zurück. Zu Kriegsbeginn wurden Wohnungen für Schlumpf-Beschäftigte gebaut, kommunikative Einrichtungen, eine große Werkskantine. Aber man vermerkt es den Schlumpfs noch heute übel, daß sie während der Besatzungszeit sowohl die Schweizer als auch die Hakenkreuz-Fahne auf den Dächern ihrer Betriebe zeigten...

parurent des cavernes renfermant des trésors. Des reporters-photographes du monde entier, avec hâte et sans choisir beaucoup, appuyèrent sur le déclencheur de leurs appareils, des nostalgiques de l'automobile tracèrent des croix sur les listes qu'ils avaient en main. Les premiers emblèmes disparurent des radiateurs. Durant ce temps, Hans et Fritz Schlumpf se trouvaient dans leur suite de l'«Hôtel des trois Rois» à Bâle, luttant sans doute avec un destin qui n'accepte plus de leur accorder une chance.

Mais prenons l'histoire à ses débuts. Fritz et Hans Schlumpf, fils d'un négociant en textiles qui était citoyen suisse, ont grandi à Omegna près de Milan, dans la même région que celui qui devait plus tard devenir leur idole, Ettore Bugatti. En 1919, suite à la mort du père, la famille s'installa dans la patrie de la mère, en Alsace, à Mulhouse. Bugatti lui aussi avait quitté Milan pour gagner l'Alsace, bien que ce fût après maints détours ...

Hans Schlumpf entra comme commis dans une banque, Fritz se retrouva

Omegna, near Milan – actually the same region where Ettore Bugatti, later to become their idol, had lived. In 1919, after their father died, the family left Italy and moved back to the mother's home, Mulhouse in the Alsace-Lorraine region. Bugatti had also moved from Milan to Alsace-Lorraine, although with a few intermediate stops.

Hans Schlumpf began a banker's apprenticeship; Fritz went to work in a brokerage. Fritz demonstrated in the early Thirties, the Depression years, that he was a slick businessman. One of his co-workers remembers "Fritz Schlumpf was considered a fabulous speculator. He climbed steadily into France's financial elite."

Hans and Fritz invested their money in stocks, and in 1938 they acquired the old wool-yarn spinnery in Malmerspach. They took advantage of circumstances: its Jewish proprietors, fearful of Nazi pressure, had to sell out quick and emigrate. Soon afterward, war broke out. With respect to social services for the workers, a good deal has been attributed to the Schlumpf brothers – but all this

Oben: Fritz Schlumpf und seine Mitarbeiter im Salonwagen unterwegs nach Mailand. Rechts: Paula Schlumpf nach ihrer Verurteilung.

En haut: Fritz Schlumpf et ses collaborateurs en route pour Milan dans le wagon-salon. A droite: Paula Schlumpf après le procès.

Above: Fritz Schlumpf and associates in salon car en route to Milan. Right: Paula Schlumpf after being sentenced.

Oben: Joviale Gesten. Fritz Schlumpf (Hintergrund) läßt zu Weihnachten einen Kinderwagen verlosen...

En haut: Un patron jovial: Fritz Schlumpf (à l'arrière-plan) donne une voiture d'enfant pour la tombola de Noël...

Above: Generous gestures. Fritz Schlumpf (in background) raffles off a baby carriage...

Während Hans keine besonderen Aktivitäten entwickelte, scheffelte Fritz immer mehr Geld. Auf diese Epoche ist man in Malmerspach, kommt die Rede auf Schlumpf, besonders schlecht zu sprechen. Man erzählt von Telegrammen an Nazigrößen, von einem Doppelspiel mit den Engländern und nie versiegendem Rohstoffnachschub für die Spinnereien.

1946 gab es einen Skandal, der durch die Zeitungen ging. Fritz Schlumpfs Ehefrau Paula, geborene Erny, mit der er seit 1935 verheiratet war, erschoß am 8. August in ihrer eleganten Wohnung am Bois de Boulogne zu Paris ihren Liebhaber, den griechischen Juden Raoul Simha, der als Finanzmann in allen Metropolen bekannt war. Nach einem fast zweijährigen Prozeß wurde die vierzigjährige Paula Schlumpf, ehedem Mannequin und Schauspielerin, zu acht Jahren Haft verurteilt.

Diese ‚Affäre Schlumpf' brachte den erfolgsgewohnten Textilkaufmann aus

chez un courtier. Durant la crise économique au début des années trente, il prouva pour la première fois qu'il était un habile commerçant. L'un de ses proches collaborateurs se rappelle: «Fritz Schlumpf passait pour un spéculateur fabuleux. Il s'est élevé irrésistiblement jusqu'à faire partie de l'élite francaise de la finance.» Hans et Fritz investirent leur argent en actions, et en 1938 ils acquéraient la vieille filature de Malmerspach. Dans cette petite ville, on raconte aujourd'hui qu'ils profitèrent du fait que les propriétaires juifs, sous la pression national-socialiste sensible également en Alsace, devaient vendre leurs installations au plus vite pour émigrer. Puis vint la guerre.

On accorde aux frères Schlumpf toute une série de mérites en évoquant les réalisations sociales pour les ouvriers – en fait si cet aspect a une réalité, il y a maintenant quelques dizaines d'années de cela. Au début de la guerre ont été construits des logements pour les

goes back decades. At the beginning of the war, apartments were built for Schlumpf employees, as well as recreational facilities and a large factory canteen.

Not too many Malmerspach citizens liked Schlumpf's idea to show the swastika flag alongside the Swiss colors during the Occupation period. Hoisting them both, the Schlumpfs wanted to make clear that they had nothing to do with *resistance* movements. Wise, perhaps, in those days, but imprudent at last...

While Hans didn't develop any remarkable activities, Fritz on the other hand raked in more and more money. When this era ist discussed in Malmerspach, Schlumpf is not spoken of in the best language: one hears tales fo telegrams to Nazi leaders, double-dealing with the English, and a supply of raw materials for the textile factory that never seemed to dry up.

In 1946 a Schlumpf scandal made the headlines. Fritz's wife Paula, whom he

Links: 1964 kam eine ganze Eisenbahn-Ladung Bugattis aus Amerika nach Mülhausen.

A gauche: En 1964 arriva à Mulhouse un train complet chargé de Bugatti achetées en Amérique.

Left: In 1964 a whole trainload of Bugattis from America arrived in Mulhouse.

Fritz Schlumpf posierte selten vor einem Wagen für Fotografen. Hier steht der Grand Patron vor einem Bugatti Typ 46S.

Fritz Schlumpf posait rarement pour les photographes devant une voiture. On peut voir ici le grand patron devant une Bugatti 46S.

Only seldom did Fritz Schlumpf pose with a car for photographers. Here Le Grand Patron with a Bugatti Type 46S.

Malmerspach nicht aus dem Lot. Er wurde Hauptaktionär der Spinnereien Erstein, Gluck & Cie. in Mülhausen und der Weberei Deffrenne & Cie. in der Nähe von Roubaix. Hinzu kamen eine Sektkellerei, das Hotel du Parc in Mülhausen und weitere Immobilien.

1972 konnte sich Fritz Schlumpf – nach Meldungen der französischen Presse – als der „sechstreichste Mann der Republik Frankreich" feiern lassen. Die Textilmonarchen des Elsaß hatten sich ihr Imperium, wie sie es die Zeitungen wissen ließen, durch „Willenskraft, Ausdauer, Geduld, Beharrlichkeit, Mut, Mühe, Sorge und Arbeit" geschaffen und gefestigt.

Fritz Schlumpf, Grand Patron in Malmerspach, war trotz jovialer Gesten wenig beliebt. Auf einer Betriebs-Weihnachtsfeier ließ er großzügig einen Kinderwagen verlosen - andererseits orderte er den Salonwagen der Schweizer Regierung, um mal eben

employés de Schlumpf, ainsi que des foyers et une grande cantine.

De nos jours encore on en veut aux Schlumpf d'avoir planté sur le toit de leur usine, durant l'occupation, le drapeau à croix gammée et le drapeau suisse. D'un point de vue économique, c'était certainement une mesure habile, mais plus tard, du point de vue politique il s'avéra que ce n'était pas fin.

Alors que Hans ne développait pas d'activités particulières, Fritz pour sa part rassemblait toujours plus d'argent. A Malmerspach, quand on parle de Schlumpf et qu'on vient à évoquer cette époque, on se heurte à une réticence certaine. Il est question

had married in 1935, shot her lover on August 8 in her elegant Bois de Boulogne apartment in Paris. The lover was the Greek Jew Raoul Simha, widely known as a financier. After a trial that lasted nearly two years, the 40-year-old Paula Schlumpf - earlier a model and actress - was sentenced to eight years in prison.

This particular "Schlumpf Affair" apparently didn't throw the successful textile merchant of Malmerspach off course. To the contrary: he became chief stockholder of the spinneries Erstein, Gluck & Cie. in Mulhouse and the Deffrenne & Cie. weaving mill near Roubaix. Other acquisitions of this period: a champagne cellar,

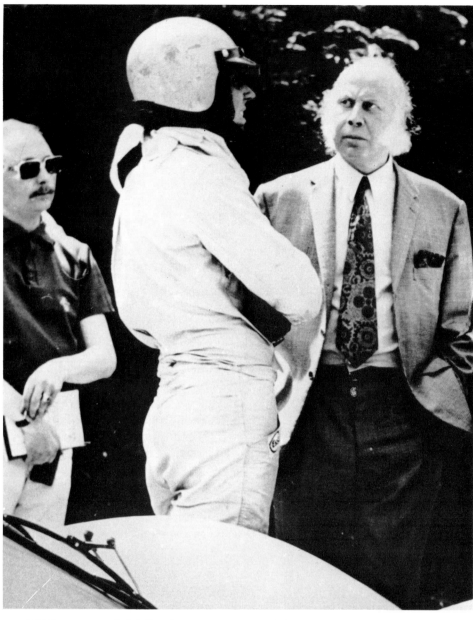

von Mülhausen nach Mailand zur Textilmesse zu reisen.

Inzwischen war das Heer seiner Feinde aus ganz anderen Bereichen weltweit angewachsen. Kein Bugatti-Enthusiast, der bei der Erwähnung des Namens Schlumpf nicht Zornesfalten auf der Stirn bekam. Eine in der Öffentlichkeit anfangs kaum bemerkte Vorliebe für die Konstruktionen seines einstigen Nachbarn Ettore Bugatti – Fritz Schlumpf war mit ihm persönlich bekannt und hatte sich in den dreißiger Jahren auf einem Typ 35 sogar an einigen Rennen beteiligt – geriet nach und nach zu einer Sammelleidenschaft ohne Grenzen. Alles, was den Namen Bugatti trug, versuchte der Textilkönig Schlumpf zu erwerben. Der Preis spielte nie eine Rolle. Vor Jahren gestand er einem Vertrauten, warum er

de télégrammes adressés à des personnalités nazies, d'un double rôle joué avec les Anglais et de sources intarissables de matières premières pour les filatures.

En 1946 il y eu un scandale dont s'empara la presse. Le 8 août, dans son élégant domicile parisien situé près du Bois de Boulogne, Paula Erny, que Fritz Schlumpf avait épousée en 1935, tuait son amant d'un coup de revolver. Il s'agissait de Raoul Simha, un juif grec connu dans toutes les métropoles comme un homme de finances.
A l'issue d'un procès qui dura presque deux ans, Paula Schlumpf, alors âgée de quarante ans, ancien mannequin, ancienne comédienne, fut condamnée à huit ans de prison.

Cette «affaire Schlumpf» ne devait pas faire vaciller le négociant en textiles de

the Hotel du Parc in Mulhouse and further real estate.

By 1972, Fritz Schlumpf was celebrated by the French press as the "sixth richest man in the French Republic." The Textile Kings had built and secured their empire, as they told the newspaper, through "will power, endurance, patience, persistence, courage, effert, worry and work."

Patron Fritz, despite occasional jovial gestures, was hardly beloved. Once, at the company Christmas party, he generously donated a baby carriage to be raffled off – on the other hand he ordered the salon car of the Swiss government just to go from Mulhouse to Milan for the textile exhibition.

All the while, the ranks of Fritz Schlumpf's enemies hat grown –

ausgerechnet der Marke Bugatti verfallen war: „Diese Autos sind alle im Elsaß gebaut worden. Dahin müssen sie auch wieder zurück!".

Jedes auch nur halbwegs interessante Modell schnappte er engagierten Bugattisten dies- und jenseits des Atlantiks vor der Nase weg. Er kaufte ganze Autosammlungen – wenn es sein mußte, per Blankoscheck – sofern sich nur ein paar Bugattis darunter befanden. Paul Kestler, Bugatti-Kenner und Historiker aus Straßburg, sagte: „In seiner Sammelwut zahlte er jede Summe und trieb damit die Preise hoch!" Bis es sich schließlich herumgesprochen hatte, daß man an Fritz Schlumpf nichts mehr verkaufen wollte, um wenigstens noch ein paar wertvolle Exemplare, wenn sie zur Veräußerung anstanden, in anderen Händen zu belassen. Schlumpfs anonyme Agenten waren dennoch überall und ließen Fahrzeuge ins große Mülhauser Sammellager transportieren, die als einmalig gelten dürfen. Die Sammlung, deren erste Stücke um 1956 herum angeschafft wurden, ließ sich am 11. April 1963 entscheidend aufstocken, als die Bugatti-Fabrik in Molsheim in die Hände des Industriekonzerns Hispano-Suiza überging. Schlumpf erhielt den Zuschlag für das gesamte bewegliche Inventar en bloc. Nicht nur Schraubstöcke mit dem Bugatti-Emblem kamen in den Besitz des Heimatpatrioten Schlumpf, sondern auch an die zwanzig mehr oder minder komplette Wagen. Prototypen und Sondermodelle waren ebenso dabei wie Ettore Bugattis persönlicher Luxuswagen – eine Royale. Mit diesem Wagen, dem sogenannten Coupé Napoleon (früher hatte das Fahrzeug einen geschlossenen Weymann-Aufbau getragen), war Ettore Bugatti nach der Befreiung Paris' in die französische Hauptstadt gefahren. Was aber keiner – und auch nicht Fritz Schlumpf – wußte: Hispano hatte noch einen großen Teil Originalmotoren und etliche andere Aggregate aus der Bugatti-Zeit zurückbehalten. Erst im Frühjahr 1977 wurden diese wertvollen Dinge dank der Initiative eines prominenten britischen Bugattisten in Molsheim den Hispano-Managern entwunden. Noch 1963 hatten die Schlumpfs geglaubt, totalen Bugatti-Kehraus gehalten zu haben.

Malmerspach, habitué au succès. Il devenait actionnaire principal des filatures Erstein, Gluck & Cie à Mulhouse, ainsi que des tissages Deffrenne & Cie dans la région de Roubaix. A cela s'ajoutaient des caves à champagne, l'Hôtel du Parc à Mulhouse et quelques autres affaires immobilières.

En 1972, selon les échos de la presse française, Fritz Schlumpf pouvait savourer sa «sixième place sur la liste des hommes les plus riches de France.» Les magnats du textile alsacien – toujours sur les rapports des journaux – avaient construit et affermi leur empire «à force de volonté, de persévérance, de patience, de constance, de courage, d'efforts, de soin et de travail.»

Fritz Schlumpf, le grand patron de Malmerspach, était peu aimé en dépit d'une allure joviale. Pour une tombola de Noël dans son entreprise, il donna une fois généreusement une voiture d'enfant – en revanche, une autre fois, il fit venir spécialement le wagon-salon appartenant au gouvernement suisse, afin de voyager plus commodément de Mulhouse à Milan où se tenait une foire textile.

Entre-temps la troupe de ses ennemis s'était grossie d'éléments d'une tout autre origine, mais cela de par le monde entier. Il n'était pas un passionné de Bugatti qui ne fronçât les sourcils de colère en entendant prononcer le nom de Fritz Schlumpf. Celui-ci, qui connaissait personnellement Ettore Bugatti et qui avait même participé dans les années trente à quelques courses au volant d'un type 35, avait pour les productions de son ancien voisin un intérêt particulier, qui au début passa presque inaperçu dans le public, mais peu à peu devint une passion sans bornes. Tout ce qui portait le nom de Bugatti, Schlumpf, le roi du textile, essayait de l'acheter, le prix ne jouant jamais aucun rôle. Il y a longtemps, il avait confié à un ami proche: «Ces voitures ont toutes été construites en Alsace; il faut qu'elles y reviennent.»

Des deux côtés de l'Atlantique, il soufflait sous le nez de Bugattistes engagés tous les modèles, même s'ils n'étaient qu'à moitié intéressants. Il

worldwide. There was hardly a Bugatti enthusiast that didn't grimace at the mere mention of Schlumpf. A predilection for the designs of his one-time neighbor – Fritz knew Bugatti personally and had even participated in a few races with a Type 35 in the Thirties – grew more and more into a collector's mania without boundary. Whatever had the Bugatti name on it, the textile king tried to get it. Price meant nothing. Once, some years earlier, Fritz had admitted to a condidant why he had fallen under the spell of the marque Bugatti: "All these cars were built in Alsace. Therefore they must all come back!"

Every halfway interesting Bugatti model on either side of the Atlantic was snapped up by Schlumpf before any other Bugattist could get his hands on it. He bought up entire auto collections, with blank checks if need be, just to get a couple of Bugattis included in them. Bugatti expert Paul Kestler of Strasbourg, put it this way: "In his mania he would pay any price – and by doing so he drove the prices up." And it went on this way until the word got around that, really, nothing else should be sold to Fritz, so that at least somebody besides him could acquire a worthwhile Bugatti or two.

But Fritz hat secret agents out buying up cars, transporting them to the big warehouse in Mulhouse: cars that well may have been unique. The collection, whose first objects were acquired in 1956, got a large transfusion on April 11, 1963, when the Bugatti factory in Molsheim was acquired by the Hispano-Suiza industrial concern. The entire mobile inventory went to Schlumpf en bloc – not just vises with the Bugatti emblem, but also the 20 more or less complete cars on hand. Prototypes and special models were among these, as well as Ettore Bugatti's personal luxury car: a Royale. It was in this car, the so-called Coupé Napoleon (earlier it had had a closed Weymann body), that Ettore Bugatti drove to Paris after the liberation of France. But what nobody – not even Fritz Schlumpf – knew was that Hispano had retained a large number of original Bugatti engines and other major components. Not until Spring 1977 were these valuable objects pirated away, thanks to

Ein Jahr später traf in Mülhausen ein Sonderzug aus Marseille, beladen mit 30 Bugattis, ein – Schlumpf hatte die berühmte amerikanische Shakespeare-Sammlung gekauft. Mit diesem Coup verfügte Schlumpf über die umfangreichste Bugatti-Kollektion der Welt. Und noch immer kamen weitere Exemplare hinzu – aus Osteuropa, aus Skandinavien, aus Holland, aus England, aus den USA, aus der Schweiz. Als Fritz Schlumpf einen Bugatti 46 in Prag nicht gegen Bargeld von einem tschechischen Besitzer erwerben konnte, ließ er ihm als Äquivalent einfach seinen Mercedes 300 da. Der Bugatti war bereits einem privaten Sammler in der Schweiz versprochen gewesen. Schlumpf war, wie so oft, auch in diesem Fall schneller.

Es hieß oft, Schlumpf sammle nur Bugattis. Das war keineswegs der Fall, wenn er auch französischen Fabrikaten allgemein den Vorzug gab. Er kaufte zum Beispiel den Panhard des Präsidenten Raymond Poincaré, einen Daimler der englischen Königsfamilie, Mercedes-Grand-Prix-Wagen, einige Maybach Zeppelin, zwei Dutzend Gordinis, De Dion-Bouton Voituretten, Rolls-Royce-Geister und Phantome – und natürlich immer wieder Bugattis. Allein vom Modell 57 vermochte Schlumpf einige Dutzend zusammenzubekommen.

Kaum eines der von Fritz und Hans Schlumpf erworbenen Fahrzeuge befand sich im Bestzustand. Mit zunehmender Größe ihrer ungewöhnlichen Sammlung sahen sich die Schlumpfs daher vor die Notwendigkeit gestellt, eine Restaurierungs-Werkstatt einzurichten. Sie entstand in den Räumen einer ehemaligen Spinnerei in Mülhausen; dort beschäftigten sich zeitweilig bis zu 30 Spezialisten mit der Herrichtung der antiken Automobile. Sie waren über ihre Tätigkeit stets zu Stillschweigen verpflichtet.

Und es gab einen Tag der ‚Offenen Tür‘, wobei diese Tür jedoch nur einigen wenigen illustren Gästen geöffnet wurde, über deren Besuch bei Schlumpfs die Mülhausener Zeitung „l'Alsace" schrieb: „Wir haben folgende Persönlichkeiten angetroffen: Seine Königliche Hoheit Prinz Bertil von Schweden, Seine Kaiserliche

achetait des collections complètes dès que quelques Bugatti s'y trouvaient – si nécessaire avec un chèque en blanc. Paul Kestler, de Strasbourg, un spécialiste des Bugatti et de leur histoire, déclara un jour: «Dans sa passion aveugle de collectionneur, il payait n'importe quelle somme, faisant ainsi monter les prix.» Cela dura jusqu'à ce que enfin on se soit mis d'accord pour ne plus rien vendre à Fritz Schlumpf afin que quelques exemplaires prestigieux au moins n'aillent pas dans ses mains quand ils seraient mis en vente. Toutefois les agents de Schlumpf, que personne ne connaissait, étaient partout et faisaient expédier vers le grand hall de stockage à Mulhouse des véhicules qu'on peut bien dire uniques. La collection, dont les premiers éléments furent rassemblés vers 1956, reçut une impulsion décisive le 11 avril 1963 lorsque l'usine Bugatti de Molsheim passa sous le contrôle du groupe industriel Hispano-Suiza. A Schlumpf furent adjugés en bloc tous les biens mobiliers. Ce ne sont pas seulement les étaux frappés au sigle de Bugatti qui devinrent possessions du patriote local qu'était Schlumpf, ce fut aussi une vingtaine de voitures plus ou moins complètes. On put noter des prototypes et des réalisations exceptionnelles, à côté d'un modèle de luxe qui était la voiture particulière de Ettore Bugatti: une Royale.

Avec cette voiture, le Coupé Napoléon (auparavant le chassis avait porté une carrosserie Weymann fermée), Ettore Bugatti s'était rendu à Paris juste après la libération. Mais ce que tout le monde ignorait – et même Fritz Schlumpf – c'est que Hispano avait conservé de l'époque Bugatti un important contingent de moteurs d'origine et nombre d'autres blocs. C'est au printemps 1977 seulement que ces objets de valeur ont été enlevés aux directeurs de Hispano à Molsheim, et cela grâce à l'initiative d'un Bugattiste anglais bien connu. Pourtant en 1963 les Schlumpf avaient bien cru avoir vidé totalement les ateliers Bugatti.

Un an plus tard arrivait à Mulhouse un train spécial venant de Marseille et chargé de 30 Bugatti: Schlumpf avait acheté en Amérique la célèbre collection Shakespeare. Ce

a well-known British Bugattist. As late as 1963 the Schlumpf had still believed they had gotten everything that was left of Bugatti.

A year later, a special train from Marseille arrived in Mulhouse. In it were 30 Bugattis; Schlumpf hat bought the famous American Shakespeare collection outright. And with that coup, Fritz now had the largest Bugatti collection in the world. But he was by no means finished yet. The Bugattis were still rolling in, from eastern Europe, Scandinavia, Holland, England, the U.S., Switzerland … Once, Fritz Schlumpf was in Czechoslovakia trying to buy a type 46 Bugatti saloon. Monetary problems arose, as the owner was not allowed to take foreign currency – so Schlumpf did not hesitate to leave his 300 Mercedes in exchange for the Bugatti. A Swiss collector, to whom the car was already promised, arrived a few days later. Too late: Fritz Schlumpf, as usual, had made the race. It was often said that Schlumpf collected only Bugattis. Not so, although French makes certainly were his preference. He bought up, for instance, the Panhard of the French President Raymond Poincaré, a Daimler that had belonged to the British royal family, Mercedes-Benz Grand Prix cars, serveral Maybach Zeppelins, two dozen Gordinis, De Dion-Bouton *Voiturettes,* Rolls-Royce Ghosts and Phantoms – and, naturally, Bugattis again and again. He managed to gather dozens of examples of the Type 57 Bugatti alone!

Hardly any of the vehicles acquired by Fritz and Hans Schlumpf were in the best of condition. Thus, as the extraordinary collection grew, the brothers Schlumpf saw the necessity of setting up a restoration shop. This they did, in rooms of an earlier spinnery in Mulhouse, and as time went on employed up to 30 specialists in the renovation of their vintage cars. All the workers involved in any kind of restoration jobs were strictly committed to keep silence.

In May 1965 there was an "Open House" at the Schlumpfs', which meant that a very few, very illustrious guests were allowed in. According to the Mulhouse newspaper *L'Alsace,* "We encountered the following

Oben: Werkssiedlung für die Textilarbeiter bei Schlumpf in Malmerspach. Unten: Demonstrationen im Oktober 1976 – Die CFDT meldet die Rechte ihrer Mitstreiter an.

En haut: Les maisons des ouvriers de l'usine Schlumpf de Malmerspach. En bas: Dès l'annonce de la vente des usines, les ouvriers et la CFDT manifestent dans les rues de Mulhouse.

Above: Housing for textile workers in Malmerspach. Below: A Demonstration in October 1976 – the CFDT informs the Schlumpf workers of their rights.

Hoheit Prinz Louis-Napoléon, Seine Fürstliche Hoheit Fürst von Metternich, den Grafen Villa di Padierna, die Herren Maurice Baumgartner, Louis Chiron, Monsieur de Graffenried ..." Aber der Bericht durfte nur einmal erscheinen. Sämtliche Fotos, die zu jenem Anlaß angefertigt worden waren, ließ Schlumpf anschließend kassieren, und er überwachte die Unbrauchbarmachung der Klischees in der Druckerei. Noch sollte kein weiteres Bild von seiner Sammlung an die Öffentlichkeit. Das war im Mai 1965.

Hans Schlumpf teilte die Autobesessenheit seines Bruders nur in

coup lui permettait de disposer de la plus importante collection Bugatti au monde. Et toujours s'ajoutaient d'autres exemplaires, arrivant de l'Europe de l'Est, de Scandinavie, de Hollande, d'Angleterre, des USA, de Suisse. Un jour que Fritz Schlumpf ne pouvait obtenir une Bugatti 46 contre de l'argent liquide, il abandonna sans hésiter sa Mercedes 300 au collectionneur tchèque, en échange. Le collectionneur suisse à qui la voiture avait été promise arriva trop tard. Comme presque toujours, Schlumpf avait été le plus rapide.

On a dit souvent que Schlumpf ne collectionnait que des Bugatti. Ce n'est absolu-

personalities: His Royal Majesty Prince Bertil of Sweden, His Imperial Highness Prince Louis-Napoléon, His Princely Highness Fürst von Metternich, Count Villa di Padierna, the gentlemen Maurice Baumgartner, Louis Chiron, M. de Graffenried ..." But this report should appear only once. All pictures that had been taken on the occasion were bought up by Schlumpf, who then oversaw the destruction of their plates in the printing plant. No picture of his collection was going to be allowed out into public light yet.

Hans Schlumpf shared his brother's madness for automobiles only to a

Oben: Das geschlossene Schlumpf-Hotel. Rechts oben die zur Hilfe gerufene Polizei-Einheit; darunter die DC-3, die ihren Platz auf dem Museumsdach einnehmen sollte.

Ci-dessus: L'hôtel Schlumpf est fermé. En haut à droite: Il a fallu faire appel à la police pour protéger les Schlumpf. En dessous: Le DC-3 qui devait être installé sur le toit du musée.

Above, the Schlumpf Hotel in Mulhouse which has been closed down. Top right, police forces as a safe-guard for the Schlumpfs; below the DC-3 – not yet converted into a VIP's restaurant...

gewissem Maße. Später wurde er zum Bremser und warnte Fritz wiederholt, es nicht zu weit zu treiben, doch da war es bereits zu spät. Statt den Maschinenpark der Textilbetriebe zu erneuern, was seit langem dringend erforderlich gewesen wäre, zog Fritz jeden nur verfügbaren Franc aus seinen Firmen und steckte ihn in seine monströse Sammlung. Löhne und Gehälter froren auf dem niedrigsten Niveau ein, sie hielten keinem Vergleich mehr im Elsaß stand. Als die Bilanzen schon ansehnliche Verluste aufwiesen, war dies für Fritz Schlumpf noch immer kein Signal, die Aufrüstung seines Privatmuseums zu stoppen oder gar einige besonders wertvolle Stücke zu verkaufen, um so das lahme Firmenschiff wieder flottzubekommen.

ment pas vrai, même si d'une manière générale il donnait la préférence aux fabrications françaises. Par exemple il a acheté la Panhard du président Raymond Poincaré, une Daimler de la famille royale d'Angleterre, des Mercedes de grand-prix, quelques Maybach Zeppelin, deux douzaines de Gordini, des voiturettes De Dion-Bouton, des Rolls-Royce Ghost et Phantom, et bien sûr toujours des Bugatti. C'est ainsi que Schlumpf avait pu rassembler quelques douzaines d'exemplaires du seul modèle 57.
Presque aucun des véhicules acquis par Fritz et Hans Schlumpf ne se trouvait dans un état parfait. Comme leur étrange collection augmentait sans cesse, les deux frères se trouvèrent bientôt devant la nécessité d'installer

certain degree. In fact, later he became a sort of brake, warning Fritz not to go too far; but it was already too late. Instead of revamping the production machinery of his textile works, which had been desperately necessary for a long time, Fritz drew every available franc out of his firms and put it into his monstrous collection. Salaries and wages in his businesses were frozen at the lowest level; they no longer could be compared remotely with the levels prevailing in Alsace-Lorraine. As his balance sheets began to show considerable losses, Fritz saw no signal to stop stocking his private museum, much less to sell off a few valuable objects, to get some capital to work saving the failing businesses.
For years, auto collectors believed that

Links: Streikparolen an der Fabrikfassade in Malmerspach.

A gauche: Slogans des grévistes sur la façade de l'usine à Malmerspach.

Left, the Malmerspach Schlumpf spinnery with strikers' paroles at the wall.

Unten: Streikwache im Garten der Schlumpf-Villa.

En bas: Un piquet de grève dans le jardin de la villa des Schlumpf.

Below, workers on guard in Schlumpf's private garden.

Oben: Der Portier des Malmerspach-Betriebes (im karierten Mantel) wird überwältigt – die Aktion beginnt. Rechts: Es wird präzise buchgeführt über die Streikwachen.

Ci-dessus: La résistance du portier de l'usine Schlumpf à Malmerspach (en manteau à carreaux) a été sans effet: la grande action commence. A droite: Un rapport précis est établi sur l'action des piquets de grève.

Above, the night porter of the Malmerspach Schlumpf works is dismissed (in chequered overcoat) – this was the beginning of all. Right, precise book-keeping of night watches by CFDT people.

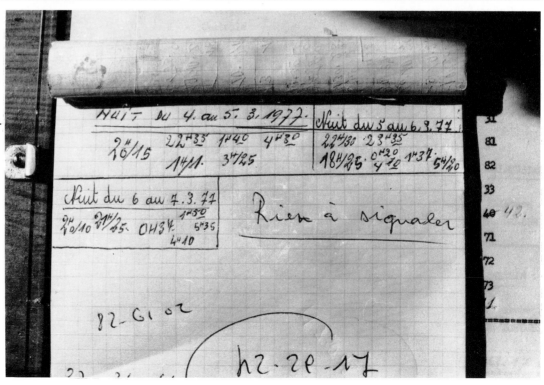

*Rechts: Die ersten Neugierigen
wollen schon in der ersten
Nacht ins Schlumpf-Museum.
Unten: Mit diesem Go-Kart um-
kreisten die Arbeiter regel-
mäßig die Schlumpf-Villa.*

*A droite: Dès la première nuit
apparurent les premiers curieux
pour contempler les trésors dans
le musée Schlumpf. Ci-dessous:
Les ouvriers se sont servis de ce
kart pour effectuer des rondes
autour de la villa dans laquelle
les Schlumpf s'étaient barri-
cadés.*

*Right, the first visitors came by
night. Below, on this go-kart
the workers drove their laps
around the barred Schlumpf
mansion ...*

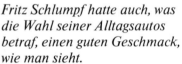

*Fritz Schlumpf hatte auch, was
die Wahl seiner Alltagsautos
betraf, einen guten Geschmack,
wie man sieht.*

*Comme on peut le voir, Fritz
Schlumpf faisait également
preuve de goût dans le choix
de ses voitures de tous les jours.*

*For his personal transportation,
Fritz Schlumpf preferred some
really distinguished motor car,
obviously.*

*Links: Demonstrationszug in
Malmerspach. „Keine Arbeit –
aber ein Museum!" lautet ihre
Anklage.*

*A gauche: Manifestation à
Malmerspach. «Pas de travail-
mais un musée», telle est
l'accusation portée.*

*Left, as soon as the break-down
of the factories was announced,
workers began to demonstrate
in the streets. "No work – but a
museum!" is their accuse.*

Jahrelang hatte es unter Automobil-
sammlern geheißen, daß die Schlumpfs
zu Lebzeiten nicht daran dächten, ihre
großartige Kollektion je einem Außen-
stehenden zugänglich zu machen. Man
sprach von einem ‚Bugatti-Mausoleum'
und kannte nicht die Zahl der darin
untergebrachten Wagen – und über-
schätzte sie oft. Anfang 1976 kursierte
das Gerücht, die Schlumpfs hätten
alles dem Staat vermacht, schon aus
vermögenssteuerlichen Gründen. Im
Februar des gleichen Jahres, so wußten
einige elsässische Zeitungen zu
berichten, sollte die Eröffnung vor der
Tür stehen, denn Fritz Schlumpf
suchte per Annoncen für seine drei
Museums-Restaurants Fachpersonal,
sämtliche Fahrzeuge wurden für die
Produktion von Farbpostkarten
fotografiert. Es gab Hotelarrangements
für auswärtige Besucher, die vor allem
aus den USA kommen sollten.
25 Francs Eintritt wollte man für die
Besichtigung der Schlumpf-Schätze
nehmen, später war die Rede sogar
von 50 Francs.

Die ehemaligen Fabrikhallen an der
Avenue de Colmar zu Mülhausen
waren zu einem Prachtbau avanciert,
was man ihnen von außen indessen
nicht ansieht. Hinter der schmucklosen
Fabrikfassade verbirgt sich kostbares
Interieur. In der Eingangshalle prangt
ein gewaltiger Lüster aus Murano-
Kristall, der sein Licht auf eine
voluminöse Barockorgel wirft.
Schlumpf hatte sie in einem öster-
reichischen Schloß gesehen und auf
der Stelle erworben. Die Gänge
zwischen den Automobilen, die auf
sorgsam mit feinem Kies zugedeckten
Podesten stehen und unter den Achsen
abgestützt werden, sind mit Mosaiken
ausgelegt. An die 500 Straßenlaternen,
die jenen auf der Seine-Brücke
Alexander III zu Paris gleichen,
illuminieren den unvorstellbar großen
Saal. Gleich am Eingang prunkt eine
Gedenkstätte mit dem überlebens-
großen Porträt der Mutter Jeanne
Schlumpf – ihr widmeten die Brüder
das Museum, und auch die ‚Haupt-
Avenue' im Saal wurde nach ihr
benannt.
Daß es im Frühjahr 1976 nicht zur
Eröffnung des Museums kam, lag
nicht an der verzögerten Fertigstellung
oder am Veto der Behörden, was die
Aufstellung der antiken DC-3, die auf

un atelier de restauration. Il fut créé
dans les locaux d'une ancienne filature
de Mulhouse. Jusqu'à trente spécialistes
y furent occupés durant un temps à
restaurer les voitures anciennes. Ils étaient
tenus de ne pas parler de leur activité.

Et il y eut une opération «porte
ouverte» au mois de mai 1965; il est
vrai toutefois que cette porte s'ouvrit
uniquement à quelques rares invités de
marque dont la visite chez les
Schlumpf amena le journal l'Alsace, de
Mulhouse, à écrire ces lignes: «Nous
avons rencontré les personnalités
suivantes: son Altesse Royale le Prince
Bertil de Suède, son Altesse Impériale
le Prince Louis-Napoléon, son Altesse

*Die belagerte Schlumpf-Villa im
Thann-Tal. Drei Tage hielten es die
Eingeschlossenen aus.*

*Le siège de la villa Schlumpf dans
la vallée de la Thur. Les assiégés ont
tenu durant trois jours.*

*The Schlumpf estate under occupation,
which lasted three days with the brothers
locked inside.*

the Schlumpfs never, as long as they
had lived, intended to open up their
collection to the outside world. One
spoke of a "Bugatti mausoleum" and
knew not the number of vehicles in it –
the number was in fact usually
overestimated. Then in early 1976,

dem Dach als Blickfang ihren Platz erhalten sollte, betraf, sondern an der Unzufriedenheit Fritz Schlumpfs über die 600 Farbfotos, die er für seine Postkartenproduktion hatte anfertigen lassen. Er ließ sich sämtliche Filme aushändigen, nicht ein einziges Bild gelangte an die Öffentlichkeit, geschweige denn in die noch immer leerstehenden Verkaufs-Automaten. Fast gleichzeitig kam es nach Jahren aufgestauter Aggressionen zu inner-betrieblichen Auseinandersetzungen. Die ersten Oktobertage des Jahres 1976 waren schließlich der Anfang vom Ende. Eine regelrechte Schlumpf-Revolution brach aus. Arbeitsnieder-legungen, Demonstrationsmärsche, Belagerung der Schlumpf-Villa. 500 Arbeiter der Kammgarnspinnerei Malmerspach bezogen Posten vor dem weißen Haus im Thann-Tal, sperrten den Insassen Strom- und Wasserzufuhr ab. In Sprechchören forderten sie: ‚Schlumpf en prison!' – Schlumpf ins Gefängnis!

Als 120 Mann Polizei, geschickt von der Präfektur des Departements Haut-Rhin, am dritten Belagerungstag die umstellte Villa freiknüppelten, hatten die Brüder Schlumpf ihre Koffer bereits gepackt. Unter dem Schutz schwerbewaffneter Gendarmen, die ihnen sogar das Gepäck tragen halfen, verließen die weißhaarigen Alten ihr romantisches Domizil. „Laßt Euch hier nie wieder blicken!" riefen ihnen aufgebrachte Arbeiter nach. „Verkauft die Autos! Das ist unser Geld!" Gemeint waren die wertvollen Oldtimer, deren Wert von Experten auf runde 80 Millionen Französische Francs beziffert wird. Aber die Verluste der Schlumpf-Betriebe hatten die 100-Millionen-Grenze schon über-schritten.

Durch ein Seitentor wurden Fritz und Hans Schlumpf unter Polizeibewachung zum Zug nach Basel gebracht. Als Schweizer Staatsbürger, die sie immer waren und blieben, suchten sie Zuflucht im neutralen Nachbarland.

Das von ihnen zurückgelassene Chaos beschäftigte seitdem höchste Re-gierungskreise in Paris. Allein im Elsaß gab es 1976 22 000 Arbeitslose, und vom Zusammenbruch der Schlumpf-Betriebe waren mehr als 6000

le Prince de Metternich, le Comte Villa di Padierna, Messieurs Maurice Baumgartner et Louis Chiron, Monsieur de Graffenried ...»

Mais le reportage dut paraître sans photos. Schlumpf récupéra toutes les épreuves tirées à cette occasion et fit savoir à l'imprimerie qu'il désirait que les clichés soient rendus inutilisables. Cette fois-là encore aucune photo de sa collection ne devait être rendue publique.

Hans Schlumpf ne partageait la passion automobile de son frère que dans une certaine mesure. A la fin, il le retint même et il lui conseilla plusieurs fois de ne pas pousser les choses trop loin. Mais il était déjà trop tard. Au lieu de renouveler le parc de machines dans ses usines textiles - une mesure urgente qui aurait dû être prise depuis longtemps – Fritz retirait de ses firmes chaque sou possible pour l'investir dans sa monstrueuse collection. Les salaires s'établirent au plus bas niveau, ils ne supportaient plus aucune comparaison en Alsace. Lorsque les bilans commencèrent à faire apparaître des pertes considérables, Fritz Schlumpf ne comprit toujours pas que c'était pour lui le signal d'arrêter l'équipement de son musée privé ou même de vendre quelques voitures particulièrement prestigieuses afin de renflouer ses entreprises en difficulté.

Durant des années la rumeur avait circulé parmi les collectionneurs automobiles que du vivant des Schlumpf il ne saurait être question que ceux-ci ouvrent jamais leur merveilleuse collection à un étranger. On évoquait un «Mausolée Bugatti» et on ignorait le nombre des voitures qui y étaient abritées, souvent même on exagérait ce nombre. Au début de 1976, le bruit courut que les Schlumpf avaient tout abandonné à l'Etat, en premier lieu pour des raisons fiscales. En février de la même année - si l'on en croit certains journaux alsaciens – l'affaire était réglée puisque Fritz Schlumpf passait des annonces pour embaucher du personnel qualifié pour les trois restaurants de son musée et que tous les véhicules étaient photo-graphiés pour la production de cartes postales en couleur. Il y eut des accords avec les hôtels pour les visiteurs qui devaient venir de

the rumor began to circulate that the Schlumpfs had already made the whole thing over to the government for tax reasons. In February of the same year, several Alsatian newspapers reported that it had gone so far that Fritz Schlumpf was placing ads for personnel for his three museum restaurants, and that the entire auto collection was being photographed for picture postcards. There were hotel arrangements for visitors, expected mainly from the U.S. The planned price of admission was to be 25 francs; later 50 francs was the talk.

What was earlier a factory space on the Avenue de Colmar in Mulhouse was now turned into an elegant structure, although this was not noticeable from the outside. Behind its plain facade, though, a costly interior took shape. In the entrance hall, a huge chandelier casts its light on a baroque organ: Schlumpf saw the organ in an Austrian castle and bought it on the spot. Walkways between the cars, which stand on platforms covered pain-stakingly with fine gravel with their axles supported from underneath, are tiled. A good 500 street lanterns, patterned after those of the Alexander III bridge in Paris, illumate the incredibly huge main hall. Right at the entrance a bigger-than-life portrait of mother Jeanne Schlumpf is the focus of a memorial: the brothers dedicated their museum to her, and its *rue principale* is named after her.

The fact that the planned grand opening did not take place in spring 1976 had nothing to do with delays in preparation of the DC-3 that was supposed to sit on the roof as a restaurant for VIP's and draw attention to the museum. No, Fritz Schlumpf simply wasn't happy with his postcard produc-tion! He took control of all the film involv-ed and not a single picture found its way to the public - much less into the post-card automats, which still stand empty.

At about the same time, after years of pent-up aggressions had built up, came the first internal strife. In fact, the first days of October 1976 were the be-ginning of the end; a proper Schlumpf Revolution broke out. Work was stopped, demonstration marches took place; there was even a siege of the Schlumpf estate. Five hundred

Ganz oben: Hotel Des Trois Rois, Basel. Darunter die Brüder Schlumpf und zwei junge Damen beim Stadtbummel.

Photo du haut: L'Hôtel des trois Rois à Bâle. En dessous: Les frères Schlumpf en promenade avec deux jeunes personnes.

Top: the Hotel des Trois Rois, Basel. Above: the Schlumpf brothers and two young ladies take a walk.

Menschen betroffen. Aber auch die Zukunft des Museums an der Avenue de Colmar ist ungewiß. Zunächst wurden die Türen auf Veranlassung des französischen Innenministeriums versiegelt.

Es begann eine hektische Zeit für Presseleute, Firmengläubiger, Automobil-Enthusiasten und -Spekulanten. Dutzende von Versuchen hartnäckiger Antichambristen, die wertvollen und geheimnisumwobenen Wagen wenigstens einmal zu Gesicht zu bekommen, schlugen fehl. „In das Museum hineinzukommen hat noch keiner von uns geschafft", sagte der Reporter der elsässischen Zeitung „Dernières Nouvelles d'Alsace", Jean-Claude Marchisio. Die Tag und Nacht streng bewachten Hallen boten selbst

l'extérieur, principalement des USA. On voulait prendre 25 Francs pour la visite des trésors des Schlumpf, par la suite il fut même question de 50 Francs.

Les anciens halls d'usine avenue de Colmar à Mulhouse étaient devenus magnifiques, ce dont toutefois on ne s'aperçoit pas du dehors. Derrière les façades nues se cache un riche intérieur. Dans le hall d'entrée resplendit un lustre imposant en cristal de Murano, qui éclaire un orgue d'aspect baroque de belle dimension. Schlumpf avait découvert ce dernier dans un

Die in die Schweiz geflüchteten Schlumpfs wurden im Oktober 1976 auf „Steckbriefen" der Arbeiter karikiert.

En octobre 1976 des ouvriers dressent des avis de recherche présentant la caricature des Schlumpf. Ceux-ci se sont enfuis en Suisse.

In October 1976 the Schlumpf brothers, already "safely" in Switzerland, were caricatured by the workers on "arrest warrants."

spinnery workers took posts in front of the white mansion in the Thann Valley, blockaded it and cut off its electricity and water supplies. They could be heard to demand in chorus, *"Schlumpf en prison, Schlumpf en prison!"*

As 120 policemen sent from the prefecture of the *Departements Haut-Rhin* were able to free the Schlumpf villa on the third day of the occupation, the brothers Schlumpf had already packed their bags. Under the protection of armed *gendarmes* that even helped them carry their luggage, the white-haired pair left their romantic domicile behind. "Don't ever be seen here again!" cried the mob of Schlumpf workers, "sell the cars! That's our money." What they meant

Wenig prunkvoll macht sich das schwere Eisengitter vor dem Museumskomplex – unüberwindliches Hindernis für Besucher und Neugierige.

Il y a peu de majesté dans cette lourde grille de fer devant les bâtiments du musée. C'est un obstacle insurmontable pour les visiteurs et les curieux.

A bit less imposing is this iron fence around the museum complex – an impassable barrier for visitors and the curious.

geschicktesten Spähern keine Chance. Stahlgitter, zugemauerte Kellerschächte, Dachfenster aus Milchglas sicherten die Schlumpf-Sammlung vor neugierigen Blicken. Nur ein Journalisten-Team wurde für seine Beharrlichkeit belohnt.

Es waren Werner Haas, Hans-Jürgen Schneider und Wolfgang Drehsen von der *Auto Zeitung,* die den ehemaligen Technischen Direktor des Werkes ausfindig machten und besuchten. Von ihm erhofften sich die drei Aufschluß über eine Möglichkeit, die Schlumpf-Schätze vielleicht doch aus der Nähe betrachten zu können. Sie berichten: „Er holt ein vergilbtes Stück Papier hervor. Den Lageplan, den detaillierten Grundriß des Museums. Aber die Ernüchterung folgt auf dem Fuß. Monsieur X (er wollte seinen Namen nicht genannt wissen) nimmt uns beinahe jede Hoffnung, als er die Sicherheitsvorkehrungen beschreibt. Hinter Mauern, Stacheldraht und Gittern sind elektrische Drähte, Alarmglocken und Suchscheinwerfer installiert. Tag und Nacht machen bewaffnete Wachmänner mit scharfen Schäferhunden die Runde. ‚Wenn die Wächter auch nur einen Schatten sehen, schießen die sofort. Einer von ihnen ist ein hochdekorierter Reserveoffizier der Armee.

château en Autriche et l'avait immédiatement acheté. Entre les voitures, qui sont présentées sur des plates-formes recouvertes avec soin d'un fin gravier et qui sont soutenues sous les axes, les allées sont tout de mosaïque. Cinq cents réverbères environ, semblables à ceux du Pont Alexandre III sur la Seine à Paris, illuminent une salle aux dimensions inimaginables. Directement à l'entrée se trouve un monument avec le portrait de Jeanne Schlumpf, plus grand que nature. C'est à leur mère également que les deux frères ont dédié le musée, ainsi que «l'avenue» principale qui porte son nom.
Si au printemps 1976 l'ouverture n'a pas eu lieu, c'est moins à cause du retard dans la préparation de l'antique DC-3 qui devait prendre place sur le toit pour signaler le musée et servir en même temps de restaurant pour les invités de marque, qu'en raison de Fritz Schlumpf lui-même, qui n'était pas satisfait des 600 photos couleur qu'il avait fait réaliser pour sa production de cartes postales. Il se fit remettre toutes les pellicules: pas une seule photo ne fut présentée au public, et a fortiori ne parvint dans les distributeurs automatiques qui aujourd'hui encore restent vides. Presque en même temps, après des années d'agressivité refoulée, des oppositions se manifestèrent au sein des entreprises. Les premières journées d'octobre 1976 marquèrent finalement le début de la débâcle. Une véritable révolution éclata, dirigée contre Schlumpf. Arrêts de travail, manifestations, siège de la villa des patrons. Cinq cents ouvriers de la filature de Malmerspach prirent position devant la maison blanche dans la vallée de la Thur, coupant l'eau et l'électricité aux habitants. En chœur ils réclamaient: «Schlumpf en prison, Schlumpf en prison.»

was about 80 million francs – $16 million or £ 9½ million – the estimated value of the collection. But the Schlumpf businesses' losses had already passed the 100-million-franc mark.

By a Sidegate, Fritz and Hans were taken to the railway station, still under police guard, where they would board a train for Basel. As Swiss citizens, which they had always been, they would seek asylum in Switzerland, a neutral country.

The chaos they left behind has kept the highest government circles in Paris busy ever since. In the Alsace-Lorraine region alone there were 22,000 jobless in 1976, and the collapse of the Schlumpf empire affected 6000. But the future of the museum on the Avenue de Colmar is uncertain too. For the time being, the French Ministry of the Interior ordered its doors closed and sealed.

Now all hell broke loose for journalists, creditors, car enthusiasts and speculators. Dozens of tries by stubborn waiters-in-the-wings to see the collection of secret, valuable automobiles simply failed. "None of us has yet got into that museum," said Jean-Claude Marchisio, reporter for the Alsatian newspaper *Dernières Nouvelles d'Alsace.* Not the most clever of scouts had a chance to get into the strictly guarded building. Steel window bars, cemented cellar shafts, roof windows of frosted glass – all measures were taken to secure the Schlumpf Collection from the curious. Only one team of journalists, as it would turn out, was to be rewarded for persistence.

They were Werner Haas, Hans-Jürgen Schneider and Wolfgang Drehsen from Germany's *Auto Zeitung,* based in Cologne. The trio sought out the former technical director of the factory

Der trifft bestimmt', klärt uns Monsieur X auf. Damit nicht genug: Alle Türen, die zu den Museumshallen führen, sind vom Handelsgericht versiegelt. Bis geklärt ist, was aus den Schlumpf-Betrieben wird. ‚Einige unserer Arbeiter waren mal sogenannte schwere Jungs', erzählt unser Mann. ‚Ich hab sie damals aus dem Knast weg eingestellt. Im Grunde zuverlässige Leute.' Was denn mit denen wäre, wollten wir wissen. Ob die nicht im Museum für uns vielleicht ein paar Fotos schießen könnten, wenn man ihnen eine Kamera in die Hand drückte ... ‚Nichts zu machen', meint Monsieur X, ‚die haben Angst um ihren Arbeitsplatz – und vor der Polizei. Wenn sie sich das kleinste Ding leisten, ist ihre Bewährung futsch.' Unsere letzte Hoffnung: der Abwasserkanal hinter der alten Fabrik. Kurz nach Anbruch der Dunkelheit sind wir mit Kamera und Taschenlampe zur Stelle. Wir bücken uns, einer nach dem anderen kriecht in das schmutzige Loch. Aber schon nach zehn Metern ist Schluß. Ein Gitter versperrt auch diesen Weg. Aus! Schlumpf hat vorerst gewonnen ..."

In den Fabriken war inzwischen der Teufel los. 1800 Arbeiter in Mülhausen, Malmerspach, Erstein und Roubaix ließen sich von den Absperrungen der Polizei nicht mehr aufhalten. Verbote und Drohungen vermochten sie nicht mehr einzuschüchtern. „Es ist Zeit zum Handeln! Auch wenn wir nicht mehr viele legale Möglichkeiten haben ..." hieß es. Die Arbeiter fühlten sich von Schlumpf betrogen. „Über eine dubiose Handelsgesellschaft hat er alle Gelder aus der Firma herausgezogen und in sein Museum gesteckt!" Louis Wenisch, Gewerkschaftssekretär im Schlumpf-Betrieb Gluck & Cie, klagte: „Daß es zu 100 Millionen Francs Schulden kommen konnte, daran ist allein Fritz Schlumpf schuld. Seit er 1971 diese Fabrik erworben hat, ließ er sich nicht mehr blicken. Aber in seinem Museum war er Tag für Tag." Die Wirtschaftsprüfer, die in monatelanger Arbeit die Ursache der Pleite analysierten, bestätigten: „Nachlässigkeit ... der Geschäftsführung" und „Zweckfremde Tätigkeit müder Vorgesetzter". Der Betriebsrat von Gluck reichte Klage ein. Durch ein Gerichtsurteil sollte

Lorsque les 120 policiers envoyés par la préfecture du Haut-Rhin dégagèrent la villa à coups de matraque, alors que le siège durait depuis trois jours, les frères Schlumpf avaient déjà bouclé leurs valises. Sous la protection de gendarmes bien armés, qui les aidèrent même à porter leurs paquets, les deux vieillards à cheveux blancs quittèrent leur maison idyllique. «Qu'on ne vous revoie plus jamais ici, leur lancèrent des ouvriers excités, vendez les voitures, c'est notre argent!» Ils pensaient à ces nombreuses voitures de prix dont les experts ont estimé la valeur à environ 80 millions de Francs français. Les pertes des entreprises Schlumpf pour leur part avaient déjà dépassé le chiffre de 100 millions.

Par une porte dérobée, la police emmène Fritz et Hans Schlumpf au train pour Bâle. Ils étaient et ils sont toujours restés citoyens suisses, aussi cherchèrent-ils asile dans ce pays neutre et voisin.

Le chaos qu'ils ont laissé derrière eux a occupé depuis les plus hauts milieux du gouvernement à Paris. Dans la seule Alsace, on dénombrait en 1976 22 000 chômeurs, et l'effondrement des entreprises Schlumpf a touché plus de 6 000 personnes. Mais c'est aussi l'avenir du musée de l'avenue de Colmar qui est incertain. Dès le début de l'affaire, le Ministère de l'Intérieur y a fait apposer les scellés.

Une époque de fièvre commença alors pour les journalistes, les créanciers, les fanatiques et les spéculateurs du monde de l'automobile. Nombreux sont ceux qui s'acharnèrent à faire antichambre dans l'espoir de voir au moins une fois les prestigieuses voitures auréolées de mystère; mais ces tentatives furent vaines. «Personne d'entre nous n'est encore arrivé à pénétrer dans le musée» déclarait Jean-Claude Marchisio, reporter des «Dernières Nouvelles d'Alsace.» Les halls étroitement gardés jour et nuit n'offraient aucune chance même aux détectives les plus habiles. Des grilles d'acier, des soupiraux murés, des tabatières en verre dépoli assuraient la protection de la collection Schlumpf contre les regards indiscrets. Une seule équipe de journalistes fut récompensée pour sa persévérance.

Streikende Werksangehörige vor dem Portal des Schlumpf-Museums.

Grévistes devant l'entrée du musée Schlumpf.

Striking employees in front of the main gate of the Schlumpf museum.

and were able to visit him. They hoped to find out if, indeed, it would be possible to see the collection closeup. Their report:

"He got a yellowed piece of paper out – the floor plan of the museum! But then came the bad news. Monsieur X (he didn't want his name mentioned) described the security measures, discouraging any hope we may have had. Behind walls, barbed wire and bars, electric cables, alarm bells and spotlights had been installed. Day and night, armed watchmen with German shepherds were making their rounds. 'If they see even a shadow, they shoot. One of them is a highly decorated reserve army officer, and he won't miss.'

"Even that wasn't all, explained Monsieur X. All doors leading to the museum halls were sealed by the court, until it could be established what is to be done with the Schlumpf holdings.

"'Some of our workers were once so-called *mauvais garçons,* boys who'd gotten into trouble. I put them to work after they got out of prison. Dependable people actually,' our man M.X tells us. What he's getting at with this, we'd like to know. Does he mean they could shoot a few photos for us in the museum if we'd put a camera in their hands?

"'Nothing doing,' says M. X, 'They worry about their jobs – and the police. If they make the slightest slip, their parole is off.' But then, he told us of

Dieser Royale-Roadster ist ein Nachbau, jedoch unvollendet. Seinem Vorbild, dem 1929 von Jean Bugatti für Armand Esders entworfenen Fahrzeug Nr. 41111, kommt er allerdings noch nicht nahe.

Ce roadster, une Bugatti Royale, est une copie qui n'a pas été terminée.

This Bugatti Royale roadster is a copy of the original no. 41 111, designed by Jean Bugatti for the Paris textile merchant Armand Esders in 1929.

Oben: Auch dieser Veritas aus Deutschland wartete vergeblich auf seine Restaurierung.

Ci-dessus: Cette Veritas allemande a attendu également en vain d'être restaurée.

Above, a Veritas from Germany, waiting for restoration. In vain, probably.

Links: Fritz Schlumpf mochte Rolls-Royce gern. Dieser Sizaire sieht ihm sehr ähnlich ...

A gauche: Fritz Schlumpf aimait les Rolls-Royce. Cette Sizaire leur ressemble beaucoup.

Left, Fritz Schlumpf had a soft sport for Rolls-Royces. Nobody knows who will ever take care for this Sizaire – looking very much like a Rolls, indeed!

bestätigt werden, daß bereits angeblich von außen hereingefloßene Investitionsmittel, die für eine Sanierung des Betriebes notwendig gewesen wären, auf nicht legale Weise ins Museum statt in die Fabriken gesteckt wurden. Einer der führenden Angestellten Schlumpfs erlaubte sich einmal, bei einem Pariser Graphologen die Handschrift seines Chefs analysieren zu lassen. Urteil: „Fritz Schlumpf ist ein lebhafter Mann mit einem schiefen

Il s'agit de Werner Haas, Hans-Jürgen Schneider et Wolfgang Drehsen de *Auto Zeitung* qui retrouvèrent la trace de l'ancien directeur technique de l'usine et lui rendirent visite. Les trois journalistes espéraient que cet homme leur indiquerait peut-être une possibilité d'admirer quand même de près les trésors des Schlumpf. Ils racontent: «Le directeur sort une feuille de papier jauni. C'est un plan, le plan détaillé du musée. Mais la

our only hope: the sewage canal behind the old factory.

"Shortly after dark: we're on the spot with camera and flashlight. We bend over, creep into the dirty channel. But after thirty feet, bars. Damn! Schlumpf has won, at least so far . . ."

In the various factories, though, it was total chaos. The police could no longer hold back 1800 workers in Mulhouse, Malmerspach, Erstein and Roubaix – there was no way to ward off what was goint to happen. "It's time to negotiate, even if we don't have many legal possibilities," was the general feeling among the workers, who naturally felt themselves betrayed by Schlumpf. That Schlumpf had guided large sums of money out of the business through a fictitious agency and into his museum was also a belief widely held.

Sollte dies etwa ein frühes Ford T-Modell sein?

Serait-ce peut-être une des premières Ford T?

Well, an early Ford model T, perhaps?

Diese prunkvolle Orgel aus Antwerpen kauften die Schlumpfs in Österreich. Ein Museumsstück, fürwahr!

Cet orgue de taille fabriqué à Anvers a été acheté par les Schlumpf en Autriche. Une pièce ... de musée!

The Schlumpfs bought this imposing organ in Austria. Truly a museum piece!

Die Postkarten-Automaten werden wohl noch sehr lange ohne Inhalt bleiben.

Les distributeurs de cartes postales resteront certainement vides très longtemps encore.

The postcard vending machines will remain empty for a long time ...

Bild von der Moral, ein Mensch, der vor jeder Verantwortung flieht und ständig darauf aus ist, anderen die Fehler in die Schuhe zu schieben. Das tut er skrupellos. Seine Charakterzüge sind von einem Hauch von Unwürde, Kälte, Grausamkeit und Herzlosigkeit durchzogen." Schlumpfs Einstellung und Egoismus wurde beispielsweise deutlich, als er an die hundert Arbeitskräfte für den Ausbau seines Museums einstellte, während seine Fabriken bereits in der Krise steckten. Er drohte der Stadt Mülhausen, mit seiner Sammlung ins Ausland zu ziehen, wenn er keine Zuschüsse bekäme. Aber die Stadt zeigte sich wenig geneigt, dem Ansinnen stattzugeben. Auch als der Einsturz des Schlumpf-Himmels zur drohenden Realität wurde, war von offizieller Seite keine Hilfestellung in Sicht, was das Museum betraf. „Wir verfügen über keine Mittel in der erforderlichen Größenordnung",

désillusion suit aussitôt. Monsieur*** (il n'a pas voulu que son nom soit cité) nous enlève presque tout espoir en nous décrivant les systèmes de sécurité. Derrière les murs, le fil barbelé et les grilles sont installés des fils électrifiés, des sonneries d'alarme et des projecteurs. Jour et nuit des hommes armés accompagnés de chiens policiers effectuent des rondes. «Même si les gardiens ne voient qu'une ombre, ils tirent aussitôt. L'un d'entre-eux est un officier de réserve hautement décoré. Celui-là, il fera sûrement mouche» nous instruit Monsieur***. Ce n'est pas tout: sur toutes les portes menant dans les halls d'exposition le tribunal de commerce a fait mettre les scellés; en attendant que soit décidé le sort des entreprises Schlumpf. «Quelques-uns de nos ouvriers ont été des casseurs, raconte notre homme, à l'époque je suis allé les embaucher en prison. Au fond, des types sur qui on peut

"That it could go this far – 100 million francs of indebtedness – is strictly the fault of Fritz Schlumpf," complains Louis Wenisch, union secretary at Gluck & Cie. "Since he acquired this business in 1971 we haven't seen him here. But he was in his museum day after day." Auditors who spent months establishing the cause of the failure confirm Wenisch: "Negligence ... of the management" and "inappropriate activities of tired supervisors." The shop committee of Gluck, in fact, is bringing suit: a court will decide if the capital needed for modernization of the works was indeed transferred to the museum by illegal means.

One of Schlumpf's top employees once allowed himself the amusement of taking a signature of Fritz's to a graphologist in Paris. The analysis: "Fritz Schlumpf is a lively man with a skewed concept of morals; a human

hieß es. Allein der Sanierungsplan für die Fabriken hätte hohe Zuschüsse wie natürlich auch Aufwendungen von seiten der Besitzer erfordert – Gelder, die keiner lockermachen wollte. Die Herren Schlumpf ließen es darauf ankommen und äußerten sich in ihrer Hotelsuite nicht mehr zur Sache. Sie suchten Zerstreuung beim Stadtbummel mit jungen Damen.

Inzwischen hatten es die Männer von der *Auto Zeitung* doch geschafft, sich Zutritt zu der Museumshalle zu verschaffen. Als erste Zeitschrift der Welt brachte das Blatt Anfang 1977 Bilder von der unermeßlichen Pracht der Schlumpf-Kollektion. Ein Ansturm weiterer Pressefotografen folgte, Betriebsrat und Funktionäre der Textil-Gewerkschaft CFDT, die es in ihre Verantwortung übernommen hatten, für die Sicherung des Anwesens zu sorgen, öffneten die Portale. In das als „Museum des Volkes" deklarierte Heiligtum quollen Tausende von Besuchern, den großen Augenblick ihres Lebens genießend ...

Die am 7. März 1977 von den Arbeitern im Alleingang entwickelte Initiative wurde aber schon 14 Tage später vom Landgericht Mülhausen durch eine einstweilige Verfügung revidiert. Jedem „Unbefugten" wurde es ab sofort verboten, den Museums-komplex zu betreten. Als letzte zogen drei Männer ab, die auch als erste „Aladins Wundergrotte", wie die Londoner Sunday Times das Museum bezeichnet hatte, gewesen waren – die drei Journalisten der *Auto Zeitung*. Was keinem ihrer französischen oder britischen Kollegen gelungen war, hatten sie geschafft, nämlich jeden einzelnen Wagen in buchstäblich aller-letzter Minute zu fotografieren. Erst später kamen weitere Fotografen-Teams zum Zuge.

Gegen die in Basel lebenden Brüder Schlumpf war Haftbefehl erlassen worden. Freilich nur in Frankreich vollstreckbar. Gleichzeitig wurden sie – erfolglos – aufgefordert, vier Millionen Francs Sicherheit zu leisten für den Fall, daß bei einer gerichtlich ange-ordneten Zwangsräumung des Museums Schaden an den Fahrzeugen entstehen könnten, wodurch die Gläubiger eine Minderung ihrer Sicherheiten erlitten. Denn nichts als

compter.» Nous avons voulu savoir ce qu'ils pourraient faire pour nous. Si peut-être ils ne pouvaient pas prendre quelques photos à notre place dans le musée; on leur mettrait l'appareil entre les mains. «Rien à faire, déclare Monsieur***, ils ont peur pour leur place, et de la police aussi. S'ils se permettent la moindre incartade, leur sursis est à l'eau.» Notre dernier espoir: l'égout derrière l'ancienne usine. Peu après la tombée de la nuit nous nous y trouvons avec une lampe de poche et l'appareil photo. Nous baissons la tête pour pénétrer l'un après l'autre dans ce trou dégoutant. Mais au bout de dix mètres c'est déjà terminé. Une grille coupe ce chemin-là aussi. Finie l'expédition! Schlumpf a gagné la première manche ...»

Pendant ce temps, les usines étaient en effervescence. Les barrages de la police ne pouvaient plus contenir les 1800 ouvriers de Mulhouse, Malmerspach, Erstein et Roubaix. Les interdictions et les menaces n'arrivaient plus à les

An alles war ge-dacht – auch an seidene Halstücher als kostbares Schlumpf-Souvenir.

Schlumpf avait pensé à tout, et même aux foulards de soie comme souvenirs.

They thought of everything – even of silk scarves as souvenirs of the Schlumpf collection.

intimider. Le mot d'ordre était «c'est le moment d'agir. Même s'il ne nous reste plus beaucoup de possibilités légales.» Les ouvriers se sentaient trahis par Schlumpf. «Par l'inter-médiaire d'une société de commerce suspecte il a retiré tout l'argent de l'entreprise pour le mettre dans son musée.» Louis Wenisch, secrétaire syndical dans la maison Gluck & Cie

being who escapes all reponsibility and always tries to put the blame for mistakes on others. He does this unscrupulously. His character traits are shot through with strains of dishonor, coldness, cruelty and heartlessness."

Fritz's attitude and egotism were clear as he hired about a hundred workers for the completion of his museum, right when his businesses were already on the brink of failure. And he threatened the City of Mulhouse to move out of the country, collection and all, if the city didn't cough up with subsidies. But the city was hardly inclined to bow to his demands, even when the Schlumpf roof was already beginning to cave in. "We do not have that kind of money," was the official position.

In any case, a reasonable overhaul of the factories would have required huge subsidies as well as large expenditures by their owners – money that nobody was about to turn loose. The Brothers Schlumpf simply let it ride and took

their chances. No comments were forthcoming from their hotel suite in Basel either; there they seemed to be seeking diversion by going for strolls with young ladies.

Meanwhile, though, the men from *Auto Zeitung* had won admission to the halls of Schlumpf, and the magazine became the first to publish photos of the incalculable splendor of the

Die Schlumpf-Sammlung ist Jeanne Schlumpf, der Mutter der beiden Textilkönige, gewidmet. Am Halleneingang prangt das überlebensgroße Porträt von Madame.

La collection Schlumpf est dédiée à Jeanne Schlumpf, la mère des deux rois du textile. A l'entrée du hall trône un portrait de Madame, plus grand que nature.

The Schlumpf collection is dedicated to Jeanne Schlumpf, mother of the two textile magnates. Her larger-than-lifesize portrait is resplendent in the entrance hall.

die Autos der Schlumpf-Kollektion bot ihnen Aussicht, jemals wieder zu einem Teil ihres Geldes zu kommen. In einer Senatsdebatte wurde der französische Minister für Kultur, M. d'Ornano, nach den Möglichkeiten gefragt, die der Staat habe, um die Schlumpf-Kollektion in seine Obhut zu nehmen. Dieses gehöre nicht in seine Befugnisse, soll d'Ornano geantwortet haben. Die Unterhaltung eines Automobil-Museums falle vielmehr ins Ressort des Staatssekretärs für die Universitäten. In seinen Ausführungen vom 16. Juni 1977 bemerkte er, Madame Alice Saunier-Seité vom genannten Staatssekretariat bemühe sich, eine Gruppe französischer Interessenten ausfindig zu machen, die das Museum en bloc kaufen könnte, da ja wegen der Ausfuhrbeschränkung antiker Automobile (die es in Frankreich schon seit einiger Zeit gibt) die Sammlung nicht an Ausländer verkauft werden könne.

Beim Entstehen dieses Buches ist die Affäre Schlumpf noch längst nicht abgeschlossen. Das Schicksal der Textilbetriebe ist ebenso ungewiß wie das der Schlumpf-Fahrzeuge. An

qui fait partie du groupe Schlumpf accusait: «Si on en est arrivé à 100 millions de Francs de dettes, c'est uniquement la faute de Fritz Schlumpf. Depuis qu'il a racheté l'usine en 1971, il ne s'est plus montré. Mais il était tous les jours à son musée.» Les experts économiques qui ont travaillé durant des mois pour analyser la cause de la faillite ont confirmé: «Négligence ... de la Direction» et «lassitude des chefs effectuant un travail sans lien avec l'activité normale.» Le comité d'entreprise de Gluck a porté plainte. Un jugement en tribunal devait confirmer que les moyens d'investissement qui auraient été nécessaires pour l'assainissement de l'affaire avaient illégalement pris le chemin du musée plutôt que des usines.

Un des collaborateurs de Schlumpf se permit un jour de faire analyser l'écriture de son chef par un graphologue parisien. Conclusion: «Fritz Schlumpf est un homme agité qui possède une image déformée de la morale, c'est un être qui fuit devant toute responsabilité et qui cherche constamment à faire endosser les erreurs aux autres. Il le fait d'une manière sans scrupule. Son caractère est légèrement entaché d'insensibilité.» La manière d'être de Schlumpf et son égoïsme devinrent évidents lorsque par exemple il engagea une centaine de personnes pour organiser son musée alors que ses usines étaient déjà en crise. Il menaça la ville de Mulhouse de partir à l'étranger avec sa collection s'il n'obtenait pas d'aide financière. Mais la commune se montra peu encline à satisfaire ces exigences. Même lorsque l'écroulement des rêves de Schlumpf devint une réalité pleine de menaces les milieux officiels se refusèrent à toute aide pour le musée. «Nous ne possédons pas de moyens d'un ordre

collection. Afterwards, other press photographers swarmed in and the shop council, along with officials of the textile union CFDT (who together had taken over responsibility for security) opened the portals to the public. Now visitors came by the thousands into the halls, having the times of their lives in the Museum of the People, as the workers had renamed it.

The initiative taken by the workers on March 7, 1977, however, was overruled 14 days later by the Mulhouse district court by a temporary restraining order. After that, no unauthorized person was to be allowed into the museum complex. The last three to leave the oversized Pandora's Box were the three from *Auto Zeitung*. And they had managed to do what none of their French or British colleagues had: photograph each single car, literally in the last minutes.

A warrant for arrest was put out for the Schlumpf brothers – a warrant that could only be carried out in France. At the same time the Schlumpfs were ordered (unsuccessfully) to put up 4 million francs as security against possible damage to the cars should the court order the museum cleared: after all, the cars were about the only thing creditors could count on to be of value.

In a legislative debate the French Minister of Culture, M. d'Ornano, was asked if it would be possible to bring the Schlumpf collection into his Ministry. His answer was reported to be that it did not come under his authority, but that such an undertaking belonged within the activities of the Secretary of Universities. D'Ornano remarked on June 16, 1977 that Mme. Alice Saunier-Seité of that office was trying to find a group of French citizens who could buy the museum *en bloc:* because of

einigen Sonntagen wurde ab Mai 1977 das Museum wieder geöffnet, und dann machte die Zerstörung eines Veteranen Schlagzeilen, der angeblich als „Warnung" angezündet worden war. Es handelte sich um einen unrestaurierten Rosengart in einem der entlegenen Abstellräumen, die mit Ersatzteilen und Schnauferlfragmenten angehäuft sind.

Die Gewerkschaftsmänner von der CFDT haben es nicht leicht. Sie müssen Tag und Nacht das Museum, das nach Ansicht des französischen Automobil-Historikers Christian Huet „Fondation Jeanne Schlumpf" heißen muß, besetzt halten, wenn sie ihren Anspruch wahren wollen. Eine Wache rund um die Uhr muß im Gebäude anwesend sein. Der Zustand, über dessen Legalität man unterschiedlicher Meinung sein kann, wird von den Behörden weder direkt noch indirekt – am wenigsen mit Gewalt – verändert. Verboten hat man den CFDT-Männern, für den Zutritt zum „Museum des Volkes" (wie sie die Schlumpf-Sammlung wiederum nennen) Eintrittsgeld zu nehmen, was auch steuerliche Probleme nach sich ziehen würde. Aber man sammelt bei den Besuchern, wenn sie das Gebäude verlassen. Die Spendierfreudigkeit soll groß sein.

Experten in ganz Europa sprechen sich gegen einen Verkauf einzelner Stücke oder gegen eine pauschale Versteigerung aus und richten ihre Appelle an begüterte Sammler, lieber einen Fonds zur Rettung des Museums zu gründen. Der französische Druckereikaufmann und Publizist Serge Pozzoli, selbst Inhaber eines Automobil-Museums, wurde zum Sprecher einer Gruppe bekannter Experten gewählt, die einen Tausch doppelt und mehrfach vertretener Modelle gegen solche vorschlägt, die in Mülhausen nicht vorhanden sind – zum Beispiel amerikanische Oldtimer, die Fritz Schlumpf nicht leiden mochte. Und es fehlt nicht an Auktionsgesellschaften, Museumsdirektoren, Classic-Car-Dealern aus Europa und Übersee, die sich ständig in Mülhausen aufhalten, ein ansehnliches Spesenkonto strapazieren und auf die Chance warten, doch noch den einen oder anderen Boliden zu ergattern. Bislang

assez élevé» déclarèrent-ils. Le plan d'assainissement pour les usines aurait nécessité d'importantes subventions, et bien sûr aussi des dépenses de la part des propriétaires; mais cet argent, personne ne voulait le débloquer. Ces messieurs Schlumpf laissèrent faire et installés dans leur suite à l'hôtel ne firent plus de commentaires quant à cette affaire.

Pendant ce temps-là, les hommes de *Auto Zeitung* avaient quand même réussi à pénétrer dans les salles du musée. En première mondiale la revue fit paraître au début de 1977 des photos des merveilles infinies de la collection Schlumpf. Une vague de photographes en tout genre s'en suivit; le comité d'entreprise et les responsables syndicaux textile CFDT qui avaient pris la responsabilité d'assurer la sécurité des bâtiments ouvrirent les portes. Dans le sanctuaire déclaré «Musée du Peuple» s'engouffrèrent des milliers de visiteurs pour savourer le plus beau moment de leur vie …

L'initiative prise le 7 mars 1977 par les seuls ouvriers fut toutefois remise en question quinze jours plus tard par une décision du tribunal de Mulhouse. Il fut immédìatement interdit à toute personne étrangère de pénétrer dans les divers bâtiments abritant les voitures. Les derniers à sortir furent les trois hommes qui avaient été aussi les premiers à entrer dans cette caverne d'Ali-Baba, pour reprendre l'expression employée à Londres par le Sunday Times pour qualifier le musée. Il s'agissait des trois journalistes de *Auto Zeitung*. Ils avaient réussi là où aucun de leurs collègues français ou britanniques n'avait abouti: littéralement à la toute dernière minute ils avaient photographié chacun des véhicules.

Contre les frères Schlumpf installés à Bâle, un mandat d'arrêt avait été délivré. Il n'a il est vrai de valeur qu'en France. Dans le même temps il leur fut ordonné - en vain - de déposer quatre millions de caution, au cas où les véhicules subiraient quelque dommage lors de l'évacuation du musée qui pourrait être décidée par le tribunal. En effet, un tel dommage signifierait une perte de valeur au détriment des créanciers, car pour ceux-ci seules les

restrictions on the export of antique automobiles that have been in effect for some time in France, the collection supposedly could not be sold to foreigners.

As this book goes to press, the Schlumpf Affair is far from being finished. The textile business's fate is as uncertain as that of the Schlumpf cars. The museum was again opened to the public for a few Sundays beginning in May 1977; then it made headlines again when one of the vintage cars was set afire – allegedly as a "warning". It was an unrestored car in one of the remote storerooms that are mostly cluttered with spare parts and hulks. It was a well-prepared venture. Press and TV people were on the scene, when the little Rosengart burnt down.

The CFDT union people do not have an easy time of it. They have to occupy the museum, which according to the French automobile historian Christian Huet must be called *Fondation Jeanne Schlumpf,* day and night if they expect to lay their claim to it. A guard must be on hand around the clock. The circumstances, about which opinions vary, are not being with by the authorities, either directly or indirectly and certainly not by force. The interfered CFDT people are not allowed to collect admission to the "People's Museum", as they call the collection; this would create tax problems in any case. But they collect donations as visitors leave the building, and one hears that the visitors are generous.

European experts have spoken out vociferously against selling off single cars as well as auctioning off the whole collection. They are directing their appeals to wealthy collectors, hoping a foundation can be formed to save the collection. The French businessman and publicist Serge Pozzoli, who owns an automobile museum himself, has been elected speaker of a group of well-known experts that advocates trading duplicated and triplicated models for cars not now represented in the museum – for example American cars, which Fritz Schlumpf couldn't stand. And there's no shortage of auction companies, museum directors, classic-car dealers from Europe and overseas, all sitting in Mulhouse stretching their expense accounts to the limit, waiting

blieben sie ohne Erfolg. Schon aber gibt es tiefgreifende Meinungs-verschiedenheiten darüber, was mit den Schlumpf-Autos zu geschehen habe, falls sie je verfügbar würden. Die Fachpresse veröffentlichte im Juni 1977 böse Briefe, die sich französische Veteranen-Clubs zuschickten, und angeblich von „offizieller" Seite beauftrage Experten schmieden „Geheimpläne". Auch Lord Montagu of Beaulieu soll, so will es die Old-timer-Branche wissen, zum Berater-Gremium gehören, das im Falle einer Versteigerung der Mülhausener Sammlung auf den Plan treten soll.

Daß Edward Lord Montagu of Beaulieu in enger Geschäftsverbindung mit dem weltberühmten Auktionshaus Christie's steht, ist jedermann bekannt. Ein weiterer Mitarbeiter des Versteige-rungs-Unternehmens, Buchautor und Motorjournalist Michael Frostick, ist seit dem Frühsommer 1977 ebenfalls dabei, alle nur möglichen Infor-mationen zur Affaire und vor allem zur Kollektion Schlumpf zusammen-zutragen. Ob sich Christie's auf eine Mammut-Auktion vorbereitet? Das Interesse an einem solchen Unterfangen teilen sie mit der amerikanischen Firma Kruse Classic Auctions, die sich schon im November 1976, als die ersten Alarmnachrichten durch die internationale Presse gingen, nach den Chancen einer Schlumpf-Auktion

voitures de la collection Schlumpf offraient une perspective de leur faire jamais retrouver une partie de leur argent.

Lors d'un débat au sénat on a demandé au ministre de la culture, Monsieur Michel d'Ornano, quels étaient les moyens dont disposait l'Etat pour mettre la collection Schlumpf sous sa garde. D'Ornano aurait répondu que ce problème n'était pas de sa compétence. L'entretien d'un musée automobile serait plutôt du ressort du secrétariat d'Etat aux Universités. Dans ses déclara-tions du 16 juin 1977 il faisait remarquer que Madame Alice Saunier-Seité, qui occupe ce secrétariat, s'efforçait de trouver un groupe français intéressé qui pourrait racheter le musée en bloc; en effet, en raison des limitations dans l'exportation des voitures anciennes (une mesure qui a été prise en France il y a déjà quelque temps) la collection ne pourrait être vendue à des étrangers.

Tandis que ce livre est écrit, l'affaire Schlumpf est loin d'avoir trouvé une solution. L'avenir des usines textiles est tout aussi incertain que celui des voitures du musée. Ce dernier a été réouvert quelquefois le dimanche à partir de mai 1977 jusqu'à ce que la destruction d'un véhicule fasse de gros titres dans la presse. On y aurait mis le feu «en signe d'avertissement». Il s'agissait d'une voiture Rosengart non restaurée qui se trouvait à l'écart dans une de ces remises qui sont remplies jusqu'au toit de pièces détachées et de morceaux de teuf-teuf. L'holocauste fut bien préparé. La presse et la télévision en avaient été informées à l'avance.

Les syndicalistes CFDT n'ont pas la vie facile. Il leur faut jour et nuit occuper le musée – qui selon l'historien automobile français Christian Huet devrait s'appeler «Fondation Jeanne Schlumpf» – s'ils ne veulent pas que leur option soit perdue. Un piquet est installé dans le bâtiment vingt-quatre heures sur vingt-quatre. Cette situation, qui prête à réflexion du point de vue légal, les autorités ne cherchent pas à la modifier, ni indirectement ni directement, et encore moins par la force. On a interdit aux gens de la CFDT de faire payer l'entrée du «Musée du Peuple» (selon l'expression employée à nouveau par

for their chance to get one or the other *bolide*. So far without success.

There is, however, already a great deal of disagreement about what should be done with the Schlumpf cars should they become available. The French automotive press published angry letters from old-car organizations in June 1977, letters describing "secret plans" supposedly being formulated in "official" circles. According to such reports, Lord Montagu is a member of an advisory committee that will swing into action should it come to an auction of the Mulhouse collection. It is well enough known that Edward Montagu of Beaulieu is closely associated with the world-famous Christie's auction house. Another member of the Christie organi-zation, author and motoring journalist Michael Frostick, has also been gath-ering all possible information about the Schlumpf affair and, especially, collec-tion. The question naturally arises, is Christie's preparing for a mammoth auction?

Christie's interest in any such auction is shared with the American firm Kruse Classic Auctions, which started looking into the prospects of a Schlumpf auction in November 1976, right after the first wave of news about the Schlumpf affair rippled through the international press; and with the famous auctioneers Sotheby's, who sent journalists Michael Worthington-Williams and Peter Roberts

erkundigten, und mit dem berühmten Versteigerungshaus Sotheby's. Die letztgenannte Firma, die – mit unterschiedlichem Erfolg – Automobilauktionen durchgeführt hat, schickte die Journalisten Michael Worthington-Williams und Peter Roberts nach Mülhausen, sobald der Zutritt zum Museum als gesichert anzusehen war. Ihr Bericht, wenn auch mit einigen Schönheitsfehlern (zum Beispiel datieren sie die Errichtung des Museums auf 1939!), erschien im Mai 1977 in der amerikanischen Zeitschrift *Old Cars*.

Die Bilder dieses Buches sprechen für sich. Aber sie erhellen auch, daß es nur ein Gerücht war, wonach Fritz und Hans Schlumpf sich ausschließlich für französische Fahrzeuge interessierten. Delage und Delahaye sind zum Beispiel ganz schwach vertreten, ebenso Talbot-Lago und DB, von Citroën gibt es ein paar armselige Kleinwagen der frühen zwanziger Jahre, man sucht vergeblich einen Turcat-Méry, einen Georges Irat, einen Rosengart, einen d'Yrsan, einen Bedelia, und selbst Klassiker wie Salmson oder Amilcar sind knapp vertreten. Und es sind auch weitaus weniger Bugattis, als es stets hieß – die Museumshalle beherbergt ihrer exakt 122 Stück, die beiden Elektro-Kinderautos mitgerechnet. Die Gesamtzahl der Automobile beträgt 427, dazu kommen eine Reihe Motorräder, Fahrräder, Pferdekarren. Die Zahl von 584 Autos, die immer wieder durch die internationale Presse geisterte, stimmt nicht. Sie wird höchstens erreicht, wenn man die Wagen mitzählt, die an diversen Stellen eingelagert sind und auf der – langen – Warteliste der Schlumpf-Restaurateure standen.

Immer noch kursieren wilde Gerüchte um angebliche „Geheim"-Schätze der Schlumpfs, die noch irgendwo im Verborgenen schlummern. Man will einen dritten Royale gesichtet haben – aber bei diesem Wagen handelt es sich um einen mißlungenen Nachbau. Das Chassis wurde vor fünfzehn Jahren angefertigt, der Motor stammt von der berühmten Eisenbahn-Serie, die vier Räder dürften jene sein, die – als Ersatzräder – den beiden Royale im Museumsbau fehlen, und die Roadster-Karosserie ist ein wenig

eux pour désigner la collection Schlumpf); d'ailleurs cela entraînerait des problèmes fiscaux. Mais à la sortie les visiteurs sont priés de ne pas oublier le guide. Celui-ci, parait-il, aurait de gros revenus.

Dans toute L'Europe les experts se prononcent contre des ventes isolées ou une mise aux enchères globale, et ils lancent des appels aux grands collectionneurs pour qu'ils créent plutôt un fonds destiné à sauver le musée. Serge Pozzoli, qu'on connaît en France comme publiciste et homme de presse, et qui possède lui aussi un musée automobile, a été promu porteparole d'un groupe d'experts en renom qui proposent l'échange des modèles en double ou multiple exemplaire contre des modèles qui ne sont pas représentés à Mulhouse, tels les voitures de construction américaine que Fritz Schlumpf ne pouvait pas souffrir. Et on ne compte plus les sociétés de vente, les directeurs de musée, les Classic-Car-Dealers venus de tous les coins d'Europe et d'ailleurs qui ont établi leurs quartiers dans la ville alsacienne, accumulant les frais généraux en attendant l'occasion de s'approprier quand même l'un ou l'autre des bolides. Jusqu'à présent, les efforts ont été vains.

Mais on note déjà de profondes divergences sur le sort devant être réservé aux voitures Schlumpf si jamais elles venaient à être mises sur le marché. La presse spécialisée fit paraître en juin 1977 des lettres mordantes échangées par certains clubs français de voitures anciennes; et des experts chargés paraît-il de «missions officielles» élaborent des «plans secrets». On raconte également dans le milieu des teuf-teuf que Lord Montagu de Beaulieu appartiendrait au groupe des conseillers appelés à faire office dans le cas où la collection de Mulhouse serait mise aux enchères. Edward Lord Montagu de Beaulieu entretient des relations d'affaires étroites avec Christie's, la fameuse maison de vente célèbre dans le monde entier; ce n'est un secret pour personne. Un autre collaborateur de la maison, Michael Frostick, écrivain et journaliste automobile, s'occupe également depuis le début de l'été 1977 à rassembler toutes les informations possibles sur l'affaire Schlumpf et

to Mulhouse as soon as it was sure they could get into the museum. Their report, marred by certain errors (for example, it says the Schlumpfs started their collection 1939!), appeared in the May 1977 issue of the American magazine *Old Cars.*

The photos here speak for themselves. But they also show clearly that it was no more than a rumor that Fritz and Hans Schlumpf were interested only in French vehicles. In fact, Delage and Delahaye are represented quite weakly, as are Talbot-Lago and DB; from Citroën there ar nothing more than a few miserable small cars of the Twenties. You would search in vain for a Turcat-Méry, a Georges Irat, a Rosengart, a d'Yrsan, a Bedelia – and even classics like Salmson or Amilcar are in thin supply.

There are also far fewer Bugattis than rumored. The museum contains exactly 122 of them, including the two electric child's cars. In all there are 427 automobiles, plus a few motorcycles, bicycles and horse carriages. Thus the count of 584 cars that was reported over and over by the press was wrong. No matter how you figure, counting in the cars stored here and there and tabulated on the – long – restauration list, it doesn't reach that number.

Rumors are still circulating about "secret" Schlumpf treasures, allegedly hidden somewhere. For instance, a third Royale is supposed to have been seen and there were even photographs published – but this is a bastard imitation at best. Its chassis was built 15 years ago, and its four wheels may be the spares missing from the two Royales in the museum; its engine came from the famed railroad series, and the roadster body is an unsuccessful fragment similar to that of the car built for Armand Esders. And a car supposed to be a Bucciali is also anything but original – only the radiator appears to be genuine. This wreck has a Mathis engine.

The "Volkswagen predecessor" that many have reported seeing is a Mercedes rear-engine car; and the fact that the bulging engine behind a Bugatti 57S is not an alternate powerplant for the Royale, but rather a steam engine, is something few visitors have noticed.

Did the Schlumpfs manage to obtain one example – if not more – of each Bugatti

geglücktes Fragment nach Art jenes Wagens, der einmal für Armand Esders gebaut wurde. Auch der angebliche Bucciali ist kein Originalfahrzeug – nur der Kühler scheint echt zu sein. Das Wrack hat überdies einen Mathis-Motor.

Der „Volkswagen-Vorläufer", den einige gesehen haben wollen, ist ein Mercedes-Heckmotorwagen, und daß der aufgebockte Motor hinter dem Heck eines Bugatti 57 S kein Alternativ-Aggregat zur Royale, sondern eine Dampfmaschine darstellt, haben bislang auch nicht viele Besucher gemerkt.

Bei einem schnellen Rundgang wird man geneigt sein anzunehmen, es fehle kein Bugatti-Typ. Selbst der Kleinwagen vom Typ 68 (350 ccm!) ist dort wie der Typ 251, der 252. Dann aber vermißt man in der Halle, die Schlumpf-Intimus Amedée Gordini (er stiftete den Brüdern eine Reihe seiner Werksfahrzeuge) als den „Louvre der Automobil-Industrie" bezeichnete, einen Typ 30 und die wichtigen Modelle 54 und 59 ... Ein veritabler Typ 28 hingegen, der selbst von Kennern oft als 44 mißverstanden wird, gehört zur Schlumpf-Sammlung wie zwei amerikanische Cord, die in einem der Malmerspacher Depots schlummern.

Auch die Legende, jeder Wagen im Schlumpf-Museum sei ein Spitzenobjekt, stimmt nicht. Wohl befinden sich vor allem die Bugattis in ganz hervorragendem Zustand, doch stehen neben den toprestaurierten Prachtwagen auch kosmetisch arg vernachlässigte, unbereifte oder halbfertige Vehikel nicht allzu großer Rarität. Was aber den Gesamtwert der Kollektion nicht mindert.

Im Herbst 1977 hatte es den Anschein, als hätten sich die Gemüter beruhigt. Das von den Arbeitern der stillgelegten Schlumpf-Betriebe wohlbehütete Museum in der Avenue de Colmar konnte täglich außer montags von jedermann zwischen 14 und 17 Uhr besichtigt werden, und es gab kein Wochenende, an welchem nicht Busladungen in- und ausländischer Touristen nach Mülhausen verfrachtet wurden – das „Musée des Travailleurs" dürfte bis zum Zeitpunkt der erneuten Schließung

avant tout sur la collection. La maison Christie's se prépare-t-elle à effectuer une énorme vente aux enchères? Tout aussi intéressées par une telle entreprise sont la firme Kruse Classic Auctions, qui dès novembre 1976, quand les premiers échos alarmants se mirent à circuler dans la presse internationale, s'était enquise des possibilités d'une vente Schlumpf, et la fameuse maison Sotheby's. Cette dernière, qui avec un succès mitigé a déjà organisé des ventes de voitures, a dépêché à Mulhouse les journalistes Michael Worthington-Williams et Peter Roberts, et cela dès qu'on a pu considérer qu'il n'y avait plus de difficultés à entrer dans le musée. Le rapport de ces journalistes, malgré quelques erreurs de détail (c'est ainsi qu'ils renvoient la naissance du musée à 1939!) a paru en mai 1977 dans la revue américaine *Old Cars*.

Les photos de ce livre parlent par elles-mêmes. Mais elles démontrent aussi qu'il s'agissait seulement d'un bruit lorsqu'on affirmait que Fritz et Hans Schlumpf s'intéressaient uniquement aux voitures françaises. Les marques Delage et Delahaye par exemple sont très faiblement représentées; il en est de même pour Talbot-Lago ou DB. De Citroën on trouve en tout et pour tout quelques malheureuses petites voitures du début des années vingt. On cherche vainement une Turcat-Méry, une Georges Irat, une Rosengart, une d'Yrsan, une Bedelia, et même des classiques comme Salmson ou Amilcar sont peu représentés. De même il y a beaucoup moins de Bugatti qu'on ne l'a toujours prétendu – le musée en renferme exactement 122, y compris les deux voitures électriques pour enfant. Le nombre total des automobiles se monte à 427; il faut y ajouter une série de motocyclettes, de bicyclettes, de voitures à chevaux. Le chiffre de 584, qu'on retrouvait toujours dans la presse internationale, n'est pas exact. On ne l'atteint même pas en rajoutant les véhicules entreposés à divers endroits et qui étaient portés sur la liste des restaurateurs au service de Schlumpf, une longue liste ...

Et toujours circulent des bruits de couloir quant à de prétendus trésors «secrets» des Schlumpf sommeillant encore en quelque lieu caché. On prétend avoir

model? A quick check through the collection tends to confirm this; even the small Type 68 (350 cc!) is there, as well as the Type 251 and Type 252. But then one finally notices in the great hall, which the Schlumpfs' friend Amedée Gordini (who donated several of his works vehicles) called "the Louvre of the automobile industry", that the important Types 30, 54 and 59 are missing... On the other hand, a veritable Type 28 – which is often mistaken even by those in the know for a 44 – is to be found here, and even two American Cords are asleep in one of the Malmerspach warehouses.

Too, the legend that every car in the Schlumpf museum is a jewel turns out not to be true. It is true that the Bugattis are generally in outstanding condition; yet next to the beautifully restored objects of splendor stand cosmetically neglected vehicles, cars without tires, half-finished cars of no great rarity. This is not to say, though, that the collection isn't tremendously valuable.

It seemed as if tempers had cooled by the fall of 1977. Anybody could visit the museum in the Avenue de Colmar, carefully protected by one-time workers of the shuttered Schlumpf works, daily except Mondays, between 14 and 17 hours. There wasn't a weekend without its busloads of domestic and foreign tourists carted to Mulhouse. Before the "Musée des Travailleurs" was then closed again on 20 March 1979, they probably counted well over 200,000 visitors. Some have estimated that

Attraktion für Schlumpf-Gäste: Champagner der eigenen Hausmarke, aus eigener Kellerei!

Un effet pour les invités de Schlumpf: le champagne à son nom et de ses caves.

Attraction for Schlumpf guests: champagne with the house label, from the Schlumpfs' own cellars.

Die Museums-Gänge tragen die Namen von Vater Carl und Mutter Jeanne Schlumpf.

Les allées du musée portent le nom du père et de la mère des Schlumpf, Carl et Jeanne.

Some museum alleys are named after father Carl and mother Jeanne Schlumpf.

am 20. März 1979 weit über 200 000 Besucher zu verzeichnen gehabt haben. Man sprach von Spenden in Höhe von 1,3 Millionen Francs, die den Museumswächtern in dieser Zeit zugeflossen sein sollen. Für je 10 Francs erhielt jeder Spender eine Solidaritäts-Postkarte – außer selbstgeschossenen Fotos das einzige Touristen-Souvenir.

Selbstverständlich beschäftigten sich die französischen Gerichte weiterhin mit der Affäre Schlumpf. Im Oktober 1978 ging eine Meldung durch die Presse, wonach der französische Kultusminister Jean-Philippe Lecat die Automobilsammlung in Mülhausen zum „Historischen Denkmal" erklärt habe – was für die Gläubiger der ehemaligen Schlumpf-Betriebe keine gute Nachricht war. Bedeutete dies doch, daß der Staat der Möglichkeit einen Riegel vorschob, die Fahrzeuge zu Geld machen zu können. Und die große Gruppe jener, die durch die Schlumpf-Pleite finanzielle Einbußen erlitten hatten, hatte kaum ein anderes Interesse, als die Konkursmasse möglichst bald zu liquidieren. Noch aber sträubten sich die Brüder Schlumpf, vertreten durch die Anwälte Lussan und Cahn, ihre „Privatsammlung" als Bestandteil der Firmenkonkursmasse anzuerkennen. Gegen ein entsprechendes Urteil, gefällt am 2. März 1977 in der Kammer für Handelssachen des Gerichts von Mülhausen, hatten sie Berufung eingelegt. Am 14. Februar 1979 wurde in Colmar end-

découvert une troisième Royale, mais dans ce cas il s'agit d'un pâle essai de copie. Le chassis a été construit il y a 15 ans; le moteur provient de la fameuse série destinée aux automotrices des chemins de fer; les quatre roues sont vraisemblablement celles qui servaient de roues de secours aux deux Royales du musée, et qui avaient disparu; la carrosserie roadster enfin est une ébauche peu réussie sur le modèle du véhicule qui fut jadis construit pour Armand Esders. La prétendue Bucciali n'est pas non plus d'origine – seul le radiateur semble être en droit de porter ce nom. Et qui plus est, l'épave est pourvue d'un moteur Mathis.

Le «prototype Volkswagen» que certains pensent avoir vu est une Mercedes à moteur arrière; et jusqu'à présent assez peu de visiteurs ont remarqué que le moteur sur cales derrière une Bugatti 57S n'est pas réellement le bloc propulseur de rechange pour une Bugatti Royale, mais bien plutôt une machine à vapeur.

Les Schlumpf ont-ils réussi à se procurer un exemplaire, sinon plusieurs, de chaque modèle de Bugatti? En parcourant rapidement le musée on est tenté de penser qu'il ne manque vraiment aucun modèle. Même la voiturette type 68 (350 cm³!) est là, tout comme les types 251 et 252. Mais dans le hall que Amédée Gordini, l'ami intime des Schlumpf (il a donné aux deux frères toute une série de ses voitures d'usine), a baptisé «le Louvre de l'industrie automobile», on remarque bientôt l'absence d'un type 30 et, ce qui est plus important, des modèles 54 et 59... En revanche, la collection Schlumpf présente un véritable type 28, que même des connaisseurs prennent souvent pour un type 44, ainsi que deux Cord américaines, qui sommeillent dans un des dépôts de Malmerspach.

De même est fausse la légende qui voulait que chaque voiture de musée Schlumpf fût un objet de toute première classe. Certes les Bugatti surtout sont dans un état impeccable, mais à côté des voitures de luxe parfaitement restaurées, on trouve aussi des véhicules dont l'aspect laisse nettement à désirer, qui sont sans pneus, qui ne sont qu'à moitié terminés et qui enfin ne sont pas d'une rareté exceptionnelle. Cela toutefois

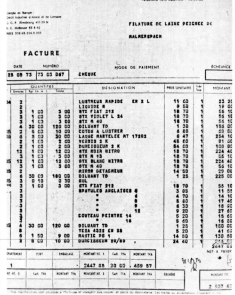

Dieses sind Dokumente, die eindeutig aussagen, daß die Schlumpfs auf Firmenkosten ihre Autos instand setzen ließen. Sie sollen als Beweisstücke dienen, daß die Fahrzeuge im Museum dem Firmenvermögen zugerechnet werden.

Ces documents montrent de manière absolue que les Schlumpf faisaient restaurer leurs voitures sur le compte de l'usine. Ils serviront de pièces à conviction pour prouver que les véhicules du musée font partie du patrimoine de l'entreprise.

These bills by a coachbuilder to the spinning factory are documents enabling the workers to prove that all cars in the collection belong to the company and are not privately owned by the Schlumpf brothers.

gültig entschieden: das Vergleichs-
verfahren der Firmen in Malmerspach
und anderenorts war auch auf die per-
sönlichen Güter von Hans und Fritz
Schlumpf auszudehnen. Das Gericht
berief sich auf Artikel 101 des Gesetzes
vom 13. Juli 1967, das eine solche Aus-
dehnung zuläßt, wenn „der Direktor
über Güter der Gesellschaft verfügt, als
wären sie sein Eigentum" oder wenn
„er einen defizitären Betrieb zu persön-
lichen Zwecken mißbräuchlich weiter-
führt". Es gab noch einen Monat Be-
denkzeit für beide Seiten – am Mitt-
woch, den 14. März aber wurde das
Urteil rechtskräftig.

Gleichzeitig hatte eine geheime Ab-
stimmung in CFDT-Kreisen stattge-
funden. Es ging um den Beschluß, die
„Besetzung" des Museums zu beenden
– die Sektion Malmerspach der Ge-
werkschaft entschied sich mit überwie-
gender Stimmenmehrheit, nämlich 75
zu 11 (bei fünf Enthaltungen), die Be-
wachung der Sammlung einzustellen.
Der Grund hierfür, so sagte Gewerk-
schaftsführer Kaspar, sei in der Zusage
einiger Firmen zu suchen, die in
Malmerspach neue Arbeitsplätze schaf-
fen wollten und fast alle arbeitslosen
Schlumpf-Mitarbeiter einzustellen ge-
dächten. Damit sei ein wichtiges Ziel
der fast zwei Jahre währenden Demonstration an der Avenue de Colmar erreicht worden.

Irgendwie ist es auch verständlich, wenn
die Aufsichtstruppe – der es übrigens
laut Gerichtsbeschluß untersagt war, die
Exponate in der Museumshalle zu be-
rühren! – nach einer solchen Zeitspanne
es einfach leid war, weiterhin den nicht
offiziell anerkannten Portier zu spie-
len...

Am 21. März 1979 übergaben Funktionäre der CFDT einem Mülhausener
Gerichtsbeamten die Torschlüssel.
Damit begann eine neue Phase der Un-
gewißheit über das Schicksal der
Schlumpf-Automobile. Noch am letzten
Tag gab es einen immensen Ansturm
auf die gigantische Museumshalle. Die
große Antwerpener Orgel – angetrieben
durch einen geschickt getarnten Elektro-
motor – schmetterte ihre Hymnen durch
den Saal, CFDT-Mitglieder stellten zum
letztenmal Papptafeln mit ihren Parolen
auf. Der Klingelbeutel am Eingang

n'enlève rien à la valeur d'ensemble de
la collection.

Durant l'automne 1977, on aurait pu
croire que les ardeurs s'étaient calmées.
Le musée de l'avenue de Colmar, bien
gardé par les ouvriers que la fermeture
des usines Schlumpf avait rendus sans
travail, pouvait être visité par tous et tous
les jours - sauf lundi - entre 14 et 17
heures. Et de fait, il ne se passa pas un
week-end sans que des bus complets de
touristes français ou étrangers ne se
rendent à Mulhouse. Le «Musée des
Travailleurs» a dû recevoir jusqu'à sa
nouvelle fermeture le 20 mars 1979
certainement bien plus de 200 000
visiteurs. On a parlé de dons pour une
valeur de 1,3 millions de Francs, qui
auraient été faits aux gardiens durant
cette période. Pour 10 Francs, on rece-
vait une carte postale de solidarité, le
seul souvenir prévu pour les touristes,
en plus des photos qu'ils pouvaient faire
eux-mêmes.

Evidemment, les tribunaux français
continuent à s'occuper de l'affaire
Schlumpf. En octobre 1978, une information circula dans la presse: Jean-
Philippe Lecat, Ministre de la Culture,
aurait déclaré la collection automobile
de Mulhouse «Monument historique»,
ce qui n'était pas une bonne nouvelle
pour les créanciers des anciens établis-
sements Schlumpf. En effet, cela
signifiait que l'Etat supprimait toute
possibilité de transformer les véhicules
en espèce sonnante et trébuchante. Et la
troupe de ceux à qui la faillite des
Schlumpf avait fait perdre de l'argent
n'avaient qu'un empressement, celui de
liquider rapidement tout cela. Les frères
Schlumpf pour leur part, représentés
par leurs avocats, Messieurs Lussan et
Cahn, faisaient encore des difficultés
pour reconnaître que leur «collection
privée» faisait partie de l'actif de faillite.
Ils avaient fait appel contre un jugement
en ce sens prononcé le 2 mars 1977 par
le tribunal de commerce de Mulhouse.
Le 14 février 1978, la décision finale fut
rendue à Colmar: la liquidation touchant
les usines de Malmerspach et d'ailleurs
devait s'étendre aussi aux biens person-
nels de Hans et Fritz Schlumpf. Le tribunal s'en référait à l'article 101 de la loi
du 13 juillet 1967 qui permet une telle
extension lorsque «le dirigeant a disposé
des biens sociaux comme des siens

donations totaling roughly 1.3 million
francs had gone to the Museum
guardians in that time. For 10 francs
each donor received a solidarity post
card, the only tourist souvenir available,
apart from self-made photos.

French courts naturally continued to
deal with the Schlumpf affair. In
October of 1978, a report appeared in
the media that France's Minister of
Culture, Jean-Philippe Lecat, had
declared the automobile collection in
Mulhouse to be "a historic monument", which was not good news for
creditors of the one-time Schlumpf
works. This meant the state had blocked
all possibility of converting the vehicles
into cash. Yet the large group of those
who had suffered financial loss through
the Schlumpf failure were solely
interested in liquidating the bankrupt
assets as rapidly as possible. The two
Schlumpf brothers, however, represented
by the lawyers Lussan and Cahn, refused
to recognize that their "private collection" formed any part of the bankrupt
firm's assets. They appealed a judgment
handed down on 2 March 1977 by the
chamber for business matters of the
Mulhouse court. A final decision was
announced in Colmar on 14 February
1978: settlement procedures for the
firms in Malmerspach and other locales
should also extend to the personal
property of Hans and Fritz Schlumpf.
The court cited article 101 od the law of
13 July 1967 which permits such
extension if "the director handles the
properties of a company as if they were
his own possessions" or "he continues
to manage a deficit business while
abusing it for personal gain". Both
parties were given a month for further
consideration but the judgment became
legally binding on Wednesday,
14 March.

At the same time, a secret vote had
been taken in CFDT circles. Its object
was a resolution to terminate "occupation" of the museum – the
Malmerspach section of the union
decided to discontinue guarding the
collection by an overwhelming majority,
75 to 11 with 5 abstentions. The reasons
for this, according to union leader
Kaspar, lay in promises made by
various firms who intend to create new
jobs in Malmerspach and plan to

dürfte sich an diesem grauen März-
dienstag noch einmal anständig gefüllt
haben.

Theoretisch hatten von nun an die
Schlumpf-Gläubiger Zugriff zu den
Museums-Exponaten – und sie müssen
dennoch warten, bis eine Reihe oberster
Verwaltungsinstanzen das Plazet hierzu
gibt. Denn noch stand die Entscheidung
im Raum, wonach der Kultusminister
das Museum unter Denkmalsschutz gestellt hatte, was gleichbedeutend mit
einem Verkaufstabu wäre. Andererseits kann es sich der Staat kaum leisten,
für rund 100 Millionen Francs (auf
diesen Wert schätzen Experten die
Autosammlung) das Museum selbst zu
kaufen. Inzwischen wurde ein Wagen
auch als gestohlen gemeldet: jener
Schuppen, in welchem unrestaurierte
Oldtimer eingelagert waren, muß in der
Nacht vom 8. zum 9. Januar 1979 aufge-
brochen worden sein, und Kenner des
Inventars vermißten einen 1938er
Peugeot Darl'Mat 402, Chassis-Nr.
705 738. Den Dieben war es gelungen,
Das Fahrzeug über die Grenze nach
Deutschland zu bringen; schon wenige
Tage später meldete sich in der Redak-
tion der AutomobilChronik, München,
telefonisch ein Leser, dem man ein
solches Auto für 15000 Mark zum Verkauf angeboten hatte. Da inzwischen
auch die Polizei eingeschaltet worden
war, kam man dem Roadster rasch auf
die Spur. Er steht heute wieder im
Malmerspacher Schlumpf-Schuppen.

Die große Affäre Schlumpf gebar auch
ihre Mini-Affären. So belangten die
nach Basel geflohenen Textilmillionäre
den Schweizer Fotografen Lienhard
wegen Veröffentlichung etlicher Bilder
in der Berner Automobil-Revue. Die
Klage wurde abgewiesen. Dann erreich-
ten die Gläubiger der Malmerspach-
Betriebe ein Vertriebsverbot des vor
Ihnen liegenden Buches in Frankreich –
eine einstweilige Verfügung ließ die
Dokumentation in ihrer ersten Auflage
zum Schwarzmarkt-Objekt jenseits des
Rheins werden. Und fast anderthalb
Jahre später reichten die Herren Kon-
kursverwalter François Dufay und
François Trensz in ihrem Namen und
in dem der von ihnen vertretenen ehemaligen Schlumpf-Betriebe auch Klage
gegen den Herausgeber dieses Buches
ein mit der Begründung, die Veröffentlichung von Fotografien der Schlumpf-

propres, ou qu'il a poursuivi abusive-
ment, dans son intérêt personnel, une
exploitation déficitaire». Les deux
parties disposèrent encore d'un mois de
réflexion; le mercredi 14 mars le jugement était rendu définitif.

Parallèlement, un vote secret avait eu
lieu dans les rangs de la CFDT. Il s'agissait de savoir si l'on allait cesser
d'«occuper» le musée. La section
syndicale de Malmerspach décida avec
une forte majorité de voix – 75 contre 11,
et 5 abstentions – d'abandonner la
surveillance de la collection. La raison –
selon Monsieur Kaspar, dirigeant
syndicaliste – serait à chercher dans la
promesse faite par quelques sociétés qui
se proposeraient de créer de nouveaux
emplois à Malmerspach et envisa-
geraient d'embaucher presque tous les
employés de Schlumpf actuellement au
chômage. Ainsi serait atteint un but
important de la manifestation qui a duré
presque deux ans avenue de Colmar.

D'autre part il faut comprendre aussi
que le groupe d'occupation – qui du
reste, sur décision du tribunal, n'avait
pas le droit de toucher aux objets
exposés dans le musée – en ait eu assez
après tout ce temps de jouer les
concierges que personne ne veut reconnaître officiellement…

Le 21 mars 1979, des dirigeants de la
CFDT remirent les clefs à un fonction-
naire de justice. Par cet acte débutait
une nouvelle phase d'incertitude en ce
qui concerne le destin des voitures de
la collection Schlumpf. Le dernier jour,
l'énorme hall d'exposition fut envahi
encore une fois par les visiteurs. Le
grand orgue fabriqué à Anvers –
entraîne par un moteur électrique
savamment dissimulé – faisait éclater
ses hymnes dans la salle, les membres
de la CFDT dressèrent une dernière fois
les tableaux de carton portant leurs
slogans. Tout laisse à penser que dans la
grisaille de ce mardi du mois de mars,
la sébile placée à l'entrée s'est une
nouvelle fois largement remplie.

A partir de ce moment-là, les créanciers
des Schlumpf pouvaient théoriquement
se rabattre sur le contenu du musée –
et pourtant, il faut qu'ils attendent; toute
une série d'instances administratives
doit d'abord donner son accord. En
effet, la décision du Ministre de la
Culture plane encore sur l'affaire: le

employ almost all the jobless, ex-
Schlumpf workers. This achieved an
important goal of the nearly two-year
demonstration in the Avenue de
Colmar.

And we can understand, in a way, that
the overseers in control – who were not
allowed to touch exhibits in the
museum hall, incidentally, by decree
of the court – were simply tired of
playing the watchman role after such a
time, particularly when it was not even
officially recognized.

Functionaries of the CFDT turned the
gate keys over to a Mulhouse court
official on 21 March 1979, opening a new
phase of uncertainty over the fate of the
Schlumpf automobiles. On the final day
there was a tremendous rush to the
gigantic museum hall. The great
Antwerp organ – driven by a cleverly
camouflaged electric motor – wafted its
hymns through the hall while CFDT
members posted slogans on their bill-
boards for the last time. The collection
box at the entrance was very likely filled
quite nicely once more, on that grey
March day.

In theory, Schlumpf creditors had access
to museum displays as of that moment –
however they still had to await approval
from a number of top administrative
offices. For the time being they were
still faced with the fact of a pending
decision by the Minister of Culture
which declared this museum a national
monument – equivalent to applying an
embargo on all sales. On the other hand,
the state can scarcely afford to buy up
the museum at roughly a hundred
million francs (the expert judgment of
the value of this car collection).
Meanwhile one car was reported stolen.
The shed where unrestored old-timers
were kept must have been broken into
during the night of 8–9 January 1979
and those who knew the inventory
found they were missing a 1938 Peugeot
Darl'Mat 402, Chassis No. 705 738. The
thieves managed to get this vehicle over
the border into Germany and a few
days later a reader applied to the
editorial offices of AutomobilChronik
by telephone. He had been offered such
a car for DM 15,000. Since the police
had also been contacted by that time,
the roadster was quickly tracked down.
Today it is back in the Schlumpf shed at
Malmerspach.

Sammlung habe deren „Neugierdewert" gemindert. Schaden: unermeßlich. Mindestens aber eine halbe Million Francs.

Auch bei Drucklegung dieser neuen Auflage ist nicht abzusehen, was mit der wertvollen Oldtimer-Sammlung in Mülhausen passieren wird. Die Telefone der großen internationalen Auktionsgesellschaften stehen wieder einmal nicht still. Sicher ist nur, daß dieses Buch, was immer aus der Fahrzeugsammlung der Gebrüder Schlumpf werden sollte, einen Katalog darstellt, dessen Wert für den Liebhaber historischer Automobile schon dadurch zunimmt, weil er die Exponate so zeigt, wie sie in den ersten Tagen zu sehen waren, als sich der Schlumpf-Tresor im Frühjahr 1977 öffnete. Sollte die Sammlung auseinandergerissen werden, wird dieses Buch zeigen, was in der Avenue Colmar zu Mülhausen im Elsaß einmal alles beieinander stand; bleibt die Sammlung erhalten, wird dem Interessierten hier ein kompletter Katalog in die Hand gegeben, der mehr als ein Bildband üblicher Art ist, nämlich die Dokumentation einer Automobilleidenschaft, deren Ausmaß zum Politikum für ein ganzes Land wurde.

BUGATTI

musée devenant monument historique, toute vente serait tabou. D'un autre côté, l'Etat ne peut guère se permettre de dépenser environ 100 millions de Francs pour racheter lui-même le musée (c'est la valeur attribuée à la collection par les experts). Entre temps aussi, une voiture a été portée volée: dans la nuit du 8 au 9 janvier 1979 quelqu'un a dû pénétrer dans l'appentis qui servait d'abri à des véhicules non-restaurés, et ceux qui conaissaient l'inventaire remarquèrent la disparition d'une Peugeot Darl'Mat 402 de 1938, numéro de châssis 705 738. Les voleurs avaient réussi à faire passer la frontière allemande au véhicule. Quelques jours plus tard, un lecteur de l'AutomobilChronik téléphonait à la rédaction à Munich pour faire savoir qu'on lui avait proposé une telle voiture pour 15 000 Mark. Comme entre temps la police avait pris l'affaire en main, on fut rapidement sur la trace du roadster.

A l'heure qu'il est, il a retrouvé sa place dans l'appentis des Schlumpf a Malmerspach.

La grande affaire Schlumpf donna naissance aussi à des mini-affaires. D'abord les millionnaires du textile, en fuite à Bâle, portèrent plainte contre le photographe Lienhard, qui est Suisse, parce qu'il avait fait paraître de nombreuses photos dans l'Automobil-Revue de Berne. Ils furent déboutés de leur plainte. Ensuite les créanciers des usines de Malmerspach obtinrent que la distribution du livre que le lecteur a sous les yeux soit interdite en France: une ordonnance de référé fit que la première édition de cette documentation devint article de marché noir sur le territoire de l'hexagone. Et presqu'un an et demi plus tard, les administrateurs de faillite, Messieurs François Dufay et François Trensz, en leur nom propre et au nom des sociétés qu'ils représentent, déposèrent plainte contre l'éditeur de ce livre en prétendant que la parution de photos de la collection Schlumpf avait diminué la valeur d'attraction de cette dernière. Le dommage? incalculable! Mais au bas mot, un demi-million de Francs...

Lors de la mise sous presse de cette nouvelle édition, on ne peut toujours pas dire quel sera le destin de la précieuse collection de voitures anciennes réunie à Mulhouse. Les téléphones des grandes maisons internationales de vente une nouvelle fois n'arrêtent pas de sonner. Une seule chose est certaine: quel que soit le sort réservé à la collection automobile des frères Schlumpf, ce livre restera un catalogue dont la valeur pour l'amateur d'automobiles anciennes est d'autant plus importante qu'il montre les véhicules tels qu'ils se présentaient aux premiers jours, lorsque les trésors des Schlumpf, au printemps 1977, se sont ouverts.

S'il advenait un jour que celle-ci soit dispersée, cet ouvrage serait le témoin de ce qui à une époque se trouvait réuni avenue de Colmar à Mulhouse; si elle reste telle qu'elle est aujourd'hui, l'amateur trouvera en ce livre un catalogue complet, qui est plus qu'un ouvrage illustré ordinaire. En effet, c'est le document vivant d'une passion pour l'automobile qui a pris pour tout un pays des dimensions politiques.

This Schlumpf super-affair also spawned its mini-affairs. The textile millionaires who had fled to Basel/Switzerland took legal action against Swiss photographer Lienhard for publishing certain pictures in Automobil-Revue, Bern. This suit was denied. Then, creditors of the Malmerspach works obtained a ban on distribution of the book you hold, in France – a temporary injunction which turned the first edition of this documentation into a black market object west of the Rhine. Almost a year and a half later the liquidators, the Messrs. François Dufay and François Trensz, also filed suit against the publisher of this volume, based on their claim that publishing photographs of the Schlumpf collection diminished its "curiosity value". Damages: incalculable, but half a million francs at least.

Even now, as this new edition goes to print, nobody can foresee what will become of the valuable old car collection in Mulhouse. Telephones are ringing once more in all major international auction firms. The only certain fact is that, whatever happens to the automobile collection of the Schlumpf brothers, this book will stand as a catalogue whose value to lovers of historic automobiles will increase from the mere fact that it shows the exhibit as it was seen in the very first days, when the Schlumpf treasure vault opened during the spring of 1977.

Should the collection be ripped apart by auctions, individual dealers or what have you, then this book will at least show what treasures once stood proudly together in the museum on the Avenue de Colmar in Mulhouse, Alsace-Lorraine. If the collection remains intact, then we offer a complete survey that is really a good deal more than just that. This is, after all, the documentation of an enthusiasm for automobiles so out of proportion that it grew into a national political affair.

Die Schlumpf-Sammlung
La collection Schlumpf
The Schlumpf Collection

Auf den folgenden Seiten sind sämtliche Exponate abgebildet, die das Schlumpf-Museum in Mülhausen zum Zeitpunkt der Entstehung dieser Dokumentation, im Mai 1977, aufwies.

Les pages qui vont suivre présentent tous les objets qui étaient exposés dans le musée Schlumpf à Mulhouse à l'époque où cette documentation a été constituée, c'est-à-dire en mai 1977.

On the following pages, all vehicles in the Schlumpf museum in Mulhouse at the time of this documentation (May 1977) are pictured.

Links/à gauche/left:
Alfa Romeo 6 C 1750 Gran
Sport compressore (Zagato)
1930.

Unten/ci-dessous/below:
Alfa Romeo 8 C 2900 com-
pressore 1939 (8 cyl.,
68 x 100 mm, 2905 cc., 2 ohc,
180 hp/5200). 1950 in der
Schweiz umkarossiert und von

Oben/en haut/above:
Alfa Romeo 6 C 1750 com-
pressore (Touring) 1934
(6 cyl., 85 x 88 mm, 1752 cc.,
2 ohc, 95 hp/4800).

Jean Studer gefahren / modifiée
en Suisse en 1950 et pilotée par
Jean Studer / modified in
Switzerland in 1950 and driven
by Jean Studer.

Gegenüberliegende Seite: Alfa
Romeo 6 C 1750 (Graber) 1932;
darunter Alfa Romeo 412
(Michelotti) 1939 (V12,
72 x 92 mm, 4492 cc.). 1952 in
der Schweiz umkarossiert und
mit Kompressor versehen.

Ci-contre, en haut: Alfa Romeo
6C 1750 (Graber) 1932; en
dessous Alfa Romeo 412 1939
(V12, 72 x 92 mm, 4492 cm³).
La carrosserie Michelotti fut
posée en Suisse en 1952.

Opposite page, top: Alfa Romeo
6 C 1750 (Graber body) 1932;
below: Alfa Romeo 412 1939
(V12, 72 x 92 mm, 4492 cc.).
The Michelotti body was replaced in Switzerland in 1952.

Oben/en haut/above:
Alfa Romeo 8 C 2900 compressore 1939 (8 cyl., 68 x 100 mm, 2905 cc., 2 ohc, 180 hp/5200). Originalkarosserie 1949 in der Schweiz durch Graber ersetzt (Fahrer Paul Glauser/Jean Studer)/la carrosserie originale fut remplacée par Graber/Suisse en

Rechts/à droite/right:
Alfa Romeo 8 C 2900 B compressore 1938/39, ursprünglich bei Pinin Farina als Cabriolet karossiert, später mit festem Dach versehen/Pinin Farina a dessiné ce cabriolet dont le hard-top fut ajouté après la guerre/this Pinin Farina bodied cabriolet got a hardtop after the war.

1949 (pilotes Paul Glauser et Jean Studer)/the original body has been replaced in 1949 by Graber/Switzerland (pilots: Paul Glauser, Jean Studer).

Gegenüberliegende Seite oben:
Alfa Romeo Disco Volante 1953 (4 cyl., 82.5 x 88 mm, 1884 cc., 2 ohc, 158 hp), Prototyp eines Rennsportwagens, Einzelstück, 1954 von Ducrey, Schweiz gefahren. Darunter: der gleiche Wagen wie links.

Ci-contre, en haut: Alfa Romeo Disco Volante 1953 (4 cyl., 82.5 x 88 mm, 1884 cm³, 2 ACT, 158 ch), prototype d'un modèle compétition. Piloté par le Suisse Ducrey en 1954.

Opposite page, top: Alfa Romeo Disco Volante 1953 (4 cyl., 82.5 x 88 mm, 1884 cc., 2 ohc, 158 hp), racing car prototype, one-off, driven by Swiss driver Ducrey.

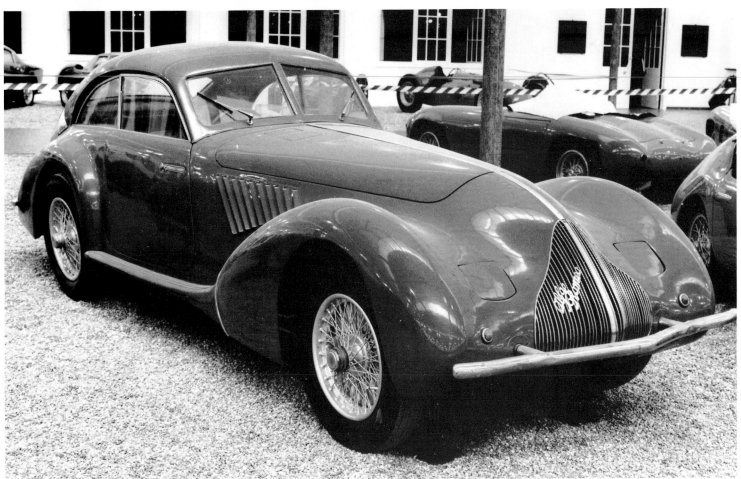

Amilcar CGS 1925 (4 cyl., 60 x 95 mm).

Amilcar C 6 Grand Prix 1926 (6 cyl., 55 x 76 mm, 2 ohc).

Amilcar CGSs 1926 (4 cyl., 60 x 95 mm).

Audi 14/50 PS K Torpedo 1924
(4 cyl., 90 x 140 mm, 3500 cc.,
50 PS/2200).

Austro-Daimler ADR 12/100 PS 1931
(6 cyl., 76 x 100 mm, 2994 cc., 100 PS/3500).

Baudier Tonneau 3 HP 1900
(1 cyl. de Dion).

46 BALLOT BARRET

Ballot 2 LT 1926
(4 cyl., 69.5 x 130 mm, 1975 cc.).

Unten/ci-dessous/below:
Ballot Grand Prix 1921 (8 cyl.,
66 x 112 mm, 2980 cc., 2 ohc).

Rechts darunter/ci-dessous à
droite/below, right: Ballot RH 2
1928 (8 cyl., 66 x 105 mm).

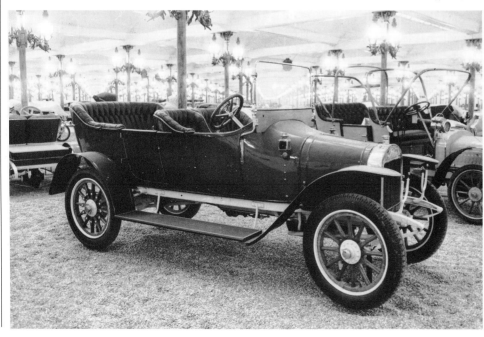

Oben/ci-dessus/above:
Barré vis-à-vis 1897 (1 cyl., de Dion).

Links/à gauche/left:
Barré Torpedo 8/10 hp 1912 (4 cyl. mono-
bloc).

Links/à gauche/left:
4.25 litre Bentley Mayfair
body 1937 (6 cyl., 88 x 114 mm,
4257 cc.).

Bentley Mk. 6 Standard Steel
Saloon 1950 (6 cyl., 88 x 114 mm,
4257 cc.).

Bentley Mk. 6 (Coach Köng/
Basel) 1949.

48 BENZ

Ganz links/à gauche/
left:
Benz Comfortable
1900 (1 cyl.,
110 x 110 mm, 1045 cc.,
3 hp/750).

Daneben/ci-contre/
inner left:
Benz vis-à-vis 1896
(1 cyl., 120 x 150 mm,
1700 cc.,1,5 hp/450).

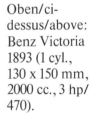

Oben/ci-
dessus/above:
Benz Victoria
1893 (1 cyl.,
130 x 150 mm,
2000 cc., 3 hp/
470).

Oben/en haut/above:
Benz Velo 1897 (120 x 150 mm,
1700 cc.,1,5 hp/450), erster
Serienwagen der Welt/la
première voiture du monde
construite en série/first motor
car produced in series.

Rechts/à droite/right:
Benz Velo 1898 mit Sonnen-
dach/à ombrelle/with
parasol.

Rechts/à droite/right:
Benz Victoria vis-à-vis 1895
(1 cyl., 130 x 150 mm, 2000 cc.,
4 hp/800).

Links/à gauche/left:
Benz 25/65 PS (6 cyl., 100 x 138 mm, 6500 cc.,
65 hp/1600). Einer der ältesten Benz-Sechs-
zylinder der Welt/une des plus vieilles Benz
6 cylindres/one of the earliest surviving
Benz 6 cylinder cars.

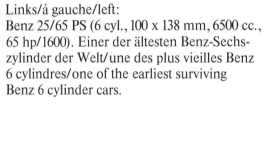

Rechts/à droite/right:
Benz Ideal 1901 (2 cyl., 5 hp
„Kontra-Motor").

Rechts/à droite/right:
Hermes/Mathis (Strasbourg)
1905 (4 cyl., 60 hp), konstruiert
von Ettore Bugatti/construite
par Ettore Bugatti/designed by
Ettore Bugatti.

Oben/en
haut/above:
Bugatti T.13
Torpedo,
1912, Chassis
no. 531.

Oben/ci-dessus/above:
Prototyp Bébé Peugeot, 1912 von Ettore Bugatti entwor-
fen/Prototype de la bébé Peugeot construit par Ettore
Bugatti en 1912, et pourvu d'un radiateur Bugatti/1912
Bébé Peugeot prototype, designed by Ettore Bugatti, with
Bugatti radiator (4 cyl., 55 x 90 mm, 850 cc., 10 hp/2000).

Rechts/à droite/right:
Bugatti T.13 competition 1912 (4 cyl., 65 x 100 mm,
1327 cc.), Chassis no. 484.

Oben/en haut/above:
Bugatti 5 litres compétition
1912 (4 cyl., 100 x 160 mm,
5027 cc.), Chassis no. 715.

Oben/ci-dessus/above:
Bugatti 5 litres compétition
1912 (wie oben/la même
qu'en haut/as above). Der
Wagen wurde auch Roland
Garros genannt/aussi appelée
Roland Garros/ also called
the Roland Garros car.

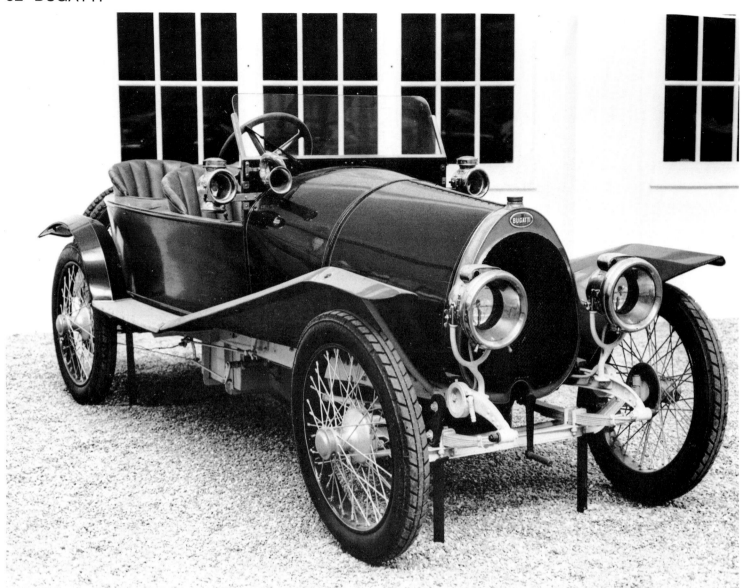

Oben/en haut/above:
Bugatti T. 13 Torpedo 1913
(4 cyl., 66 x 100 mm, 1368 cc.) –
Karosserie nicht original/
carrosserie non d'origine/body
not original. Chassis no. 765.

Rechts/à droite/right:
Bugatti T. 13 compétition mit
Kühler vom Typ 30/avec
radiateur de la T. 30/with T. 30
radiator – 1923? (4 cyl.,
66 x 100 mm, 1368 cc.). Chassis
no. 2385.

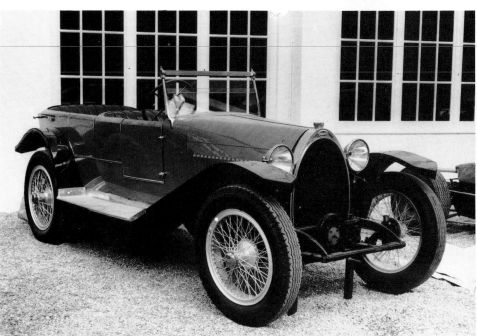

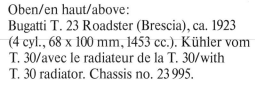

Oben/en haut/above:
Bugatti T. 23 Roadster (Brescia), ca. 1923
(4 cyl., 68 x 100 mm, 1453 cc.). Kühler vom
T. 30/avec le radiateur de la T. 30/with
T. 30 radiator. Chassis no. 23 995.

Oben/ci-dessus/above:
Bugatti T. 28 Prototype 1921, Salon de l'Auto
Paris 1921 (8 cyl., 69 x 100 mm, 2995 cc.).

Rechts/à droite/right:
Ein weiterer Bugatti T. 23 als Chassis
mit Motorhaube/une autre Bugatti
T. 23, chassis et capot/another
T. 23 Bugatti, just the chassis with
bonnet.

Links/à gauche/left:
Bugatti T. 32 Grand Prix „Tank"
1923 (8 cyl., 60 x 88 mm,
1991 cc.), Chassis no. 1461.

Rechts/à droite/right:
Die Stromlinien-Karosserie
des T. 32 war die erste, die bei
Bugatti in Molsheim gebaut
wurde/la carrosserie aérody-
namique du modèle T. 32
était la première du genre
fabriquée à Molsheim/the
body of this streamlined T. 32
Bugatti was the first to be
produced in the Molsheim
factory.

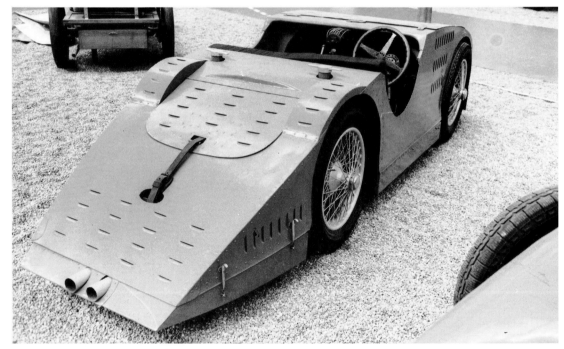

Links/à gauche/left:
Bugatti T. 35 Grand Prix,
1924–30 (8 cyl., 60 x 88 mm,
1991 cc.), mit veränderter
Motorhaube/capot modi-
fié/with altered bonnet. Chassis
no. 4565.

Unten/ci-dessous/below:
Bugatti T. 35 B Grand Prix
(60 x 100 mm, 2262 cc., mit
Kompressor/à compres-
seur/with supercharger). Mög-
licherweise T. 35/35 A/peut-
être une T. 35/35 A/perhaps a
T. 35/35 A.

Oben/en haut/above:
Bugatti T. 35 Grand Prix
1924–30 (mit Drahtspeichen-
rädern/roues fil/with wire
wheels), Chassis no. 4492.

Links/à gauche/left:
Bugatti T. 55 Roadster 1933/34
(Motor/moteur/engine: T. 44,
8 cyl., 69 x 100 mm, 2991 cc.),
Chassis no. 55 218.

Oben/en haut/above:
Bugatti T. 35 Grand Prix
1924-30 (8 cyl., 60 x 88 mm,
1991 cc.).

Oben/ci-dessus/above:
Bugatti T. 38 Touring sport
1927 (8 cyl., 60 x 88 mm,
1991 cc., ca. 70 hp/4000).

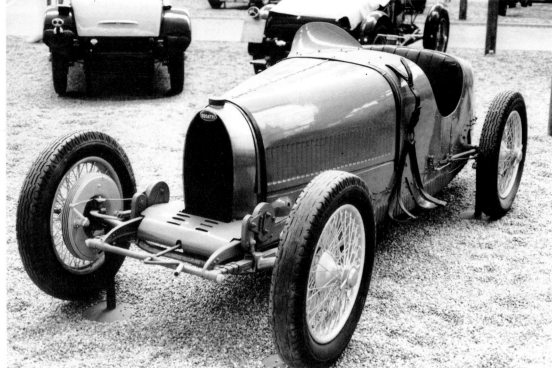

Rechts/à droite/right:
Bugatti T. 35 A 1926 (8 cyl.,
60 x 88 mm, 1991 cc., ca. 75 hp/
4000), Chassis no. 4753.

Bugatti T. 35 „Imitation" 1927
(8 cyl., 60 x 88 mm, 1991 cc.,
ca. 70 hp/4000).

Oben/en haut/above:
Bugatti T. 35 B/Chassis T. 37
(8 cyl., 60 x 100 mm, 2262 cc.),
Chassis no. 37 328.

Links/à gauche/left:
Bugatti T. 35 C 1930
(60 x 88 mm, 1991 cc., mit
Kompressor/à compresseur/
with supercharger).

Links/à gauche/left:
Bugatti T. 35 A „Imitation"
Roadster 1929/30 (60 x 88 mm,
1991 cc.), Chassis no. 4868.

Oben/en haut/above:
Bugatti T. 37 A Grand Prix 1927
(4 cyl., 69 x 100 mm, 1496 cc., 100 hp/
5500 mit Kompressor/à compres-
seur/with supercharger), Chassis
no. 373.

Rechts/à droite/right:
Bugatti T. 37 compétition 1926
(4 cyl., 69 x 100 mm, 1496 cc., 100 hp/
5500), Chassis no. 196.

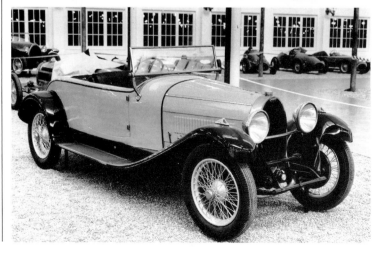

Links/à gauche/left:
Bugatti T. 38 Tourer 1927
(8 cyl., 60 x 88 mm, 1991 cc.,
70 hp/4000), Chassis no. 38 404

Gegenüberliegende Seite/
page suivante/opposite page:
Bugatti T. 40 Fiacre Coupé
1928 (4 cyl., 69 x 100 mm,
1496 cc., 45 hp), Chassis
no. 40 689.

Rechts unten/en bas, à droite/
right, below:
Bugatti T. 40 1928 (4 cyl.,
69 x 100 mm, 1496 cc., 50 hp).

Mit diesem Wagen durch-
querte Capt. Loiseau 1929 die
Sahara. Damals hatte das
Auto breite Trittbretter und
keine Kotflügel/avec cette voiture, le Capitaine Loiseau tra-
versa le Sahara en 1929. La
Bugatti avait de larges marche-
pieds, mais n'avait pas d'ailes/
in this car, Capt. Loiseau
crossed the Sahara desert in
1929. Originally the car had no
mud-guards but wide running
boards. Chassis no. 40 811.

Links/à gauche/left:
Bugatti T. 37 compétition 1927
(4 cyl., 69 x 100 mm, 1496 cc.,
70 hp/5000), Chassis no. 314.

Rechts/à droite/right:
Bugatti T. 40 Chassis 1929 (4 cyl.,
69 x 100 mm, 1496 cc., 45 hp/
3700). Räder nicht original/
roues non d'origine/wheels not
original. Chassis no. 40 343.

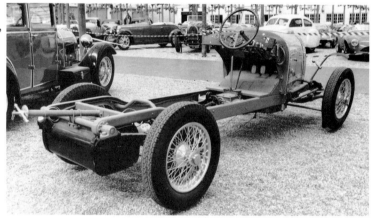

Unten/ci-dessous/below:
Bugatti T. 40 A Touring Roadster 1930 (4 cyl., 72 x 100 mm,
1672 cc., 50 hp), Chassis no. 673.

Links/à gauche/left:
Bugatti T. 40 als viertürige
Limousine/berline 4 portes/
four-door saloon 1929 (4 cyl.,
69 x 100 mm, 1496 cc., 45 hp/
3700), Chassis no. 40 524.

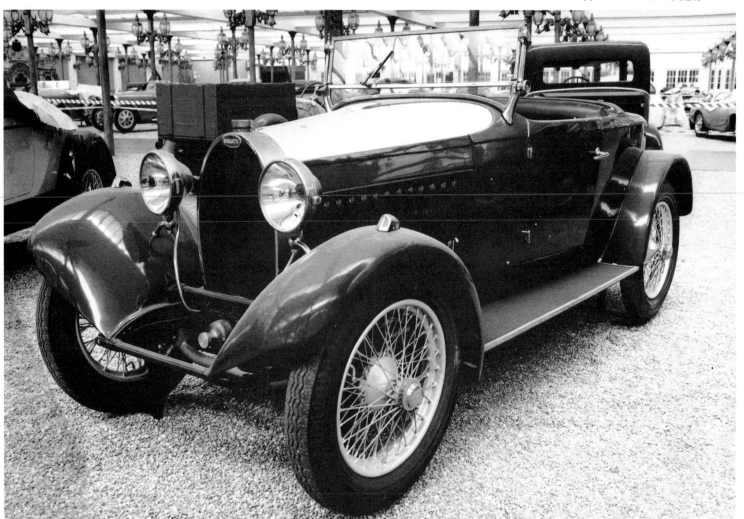

Ein weiteres Exemplar des
Bugatti T. 40 1930/une autre
Bugatti T. 40, décapotable de
1930/another 1930 Bugatti T. 40

drophead with dickey seat.
Chassis no. 40 230.

Bugatti T. 41 Royale, Chassis-Nr. 41 131. Dieser Wagen wurde 1933 im Auftrage des Capt. C. W. Foster bei Park Ward, London, karossiert, trug das Kennzeichen ALB2 und wurde von Schlumpf (mit 31 anderen Bugattis) dem Amerikaner John Shakespeare 1964 abgekauft.

Bugatti T. 41 Royale, châssis no. 41 131. Cette voiture fut carrossée par Park Ward à Londres pour le Capitaine C. W. Forster en 1933. Le numéro d'immatriculation était ALB2. En 1964, la Bugatti Royale (et 31 autres) fut vendue par l'Américain John Shakespeare à Fritz Schlumpf.

Bugatti T. 41 Royale, Limousine Park Ward, 1933 (8 cyl., 125 x 130 mm, 12 763 cc., 200 hp/2000).

This Bugatti T. 41 Royale, chassis no. 41 131, was sold to Capt. C. W. Foster in 1933. The coachwork has been made by Park Ward, London. The mighty car with the registration number ALB2 was later sold to the American John Shakespeare; his collection of 32 Bugattis was taken over by Fritz Schlumpf in 1964.

Der Bugatti Royale mit der Chassis-Nr. 41 100 war der Prototyp dieser Baureihe und trug zuerst einen offenen Tourenwagen-Aufbau eines Packard. 1928/29 wurde er zweimal umkarossiert und erhielt seltsame Postkutschen-Aufbauten mit zwei und vier Türen; dann entwarf Weymann eine hübsche Coupé-Karosse. Der Wagen wurde nach einem Unfall total neu aufgebaut, mit neuem Fahrgestell versehen (wieder Nr. 41 100) und bekam eine von Jean Bugatti gezeichnete Coupé-Karosse. Dieses „Coupé Napoleon" blieb bis zum Verkauf der Bugatti-Werke Molsheim an Hispano-Suiza in Familienbesitz.

Le châssis du prototype de la Bugatti Royale, numéro 41 100, porta quatre caisses différentes. En 1926, c'était une torpédo, en 1928 un coupe-chaise, en 1929 une berline et enfin un Coach Weymann. Après un accident, Ettore Bugatti fit construire un nouveau châssis, qui porta également le numéro 41 100. La carrosserie fut dessinée par Jean Bugatti – il s'agit du Coupé Napoléon. La voiture resta dans la famille Bugatti jusqu'au transfert de l'usine de Molsheim à Hispano-Suiza.

The Royale prototype chassis no. 41 100 had four different bodies in its first life. First a 1926 Packard touring body, followed by two curious two-door and four-door berlines, to be displaced by a nice Weymann body in 1930. After a bad crash, Bugatti designed a new chassis for his Royale, but with the same number 41 100, and Jean designed this coupé, called Coupé Napoléon. The car belonged to the Bugatti family for many years, until the Molsheim factory was taken over by Hispano-Suiza.

Oben links/en haut, à gauche/above, left:
Bugatti T. 43 Sport Cabriolet 1930 (8 cyl., 60 x 100 mm, 2231 cc., 125 hp mit Kompressor/à compresseur/with supercharger. Chassis no. 43 173.

Oben/en haut/above:
Bugatti T. 43. Chassis no. 43 298.

Oben/ci-dessus/above:
Bugatti T. 43 Roadster (Karosserie Graber) 1931, Chassis no. 43 258.

Rechts/à droite/right:
Bugatti T. 43 Torpédo Grand Sport 1928. Chassis no. 43 227.

Rechts/à droite/right:
Bugatti T. 43 Torpédo Grand
Sport 1928. Chassis no. 43 206.

Links/à gauche/left:
Bugatti T. 43 A Torpédo Roadster 1931 (8 cyl., 60 x 100 mm,
2231 cc., mit Kompressor/à
compresseur/with supercharger). Im amerikanischen Stil/
Style américain/American
style body. Chassis no. 43 A 267.

Oben/ci-dessus/above:
Bugatti T. 43 Roadster 1930.

Rechts/à droite/right:
Bugatti T. 43 A Torpedo Roadster 1931; derselbe Wagen wie
oben/la même voiture que
ci-dessus/same car as above.

Links/à gauche/left:
Bugatti T. 43 A Grand Sport
1928, Carrosserie T. 43 (8 cyl.,
60 x 100 mm, 2261 cc., mit
Kompressor/à compres-
seur/with supercharger),
Chassis no. 43A213.

Unten/ci-dessous/below:
derselbe Bugatti T. 43 wie
oben/la même voiture qu'en
haut/same car as above.

Rechts/à droite/right:
Bugatti T. 43 Roadster 1928.
Chassis no. 43 226.

Oben/en haut/above:
Bugatti T. 45 compétition 1929
(16 cyl., 60 x 84 mm, 3798 cc.,
270 hp/5000 mit 2 Kompresso-
ren/2 compresseurs/with
2 superchargers), Chassis no.
47156. Von diesem Fahrzeug
wurden nur zwei Exemplare
hergestellt/il n'y a que deux
exemplaires de ce modèle/
only two T. 45 were built.

Rechts/à droite/right:
Bugatti T. 46 Berline 1929 (8 cyl.,
81 x 130 mm, 5359 cc., 140 hp/
3500), Chassis no. 46574. Der
schönste T. 46 der Sammlung/
la plus belle T. 46 de la collec-
tion/the most beautiful T. 46 in
the collection.

Rechts/à droite/right:
Bugatti T. 44 Coupé Fiacre
1929 (8 cyl., 69 x 100 mm,
2991 cc.). Chassis no. 441 205.

Unten/ci-dessous/below:
Bugatti T. 46 Limousine
„Petite Royale" 1932 (8 cyl.,
81 x 130 mm, 5359 cc.). Chassis
no. 46 188.

Oben rechts/ci-dessus, à droite/
above, right:
Bugatti Boot „You-You", während des Krieges entwickelt/
la barque «You You», dévelop-
pée pendant la guerre/motor
launch "You You", designed
during the war (1 cyl.)

Rechts/à droite/right:
Bugatti T. 46 Coach surprofilé
(Jean Bugatti) 1935 (8 cyl.,
81 x 130 mm, 5359 cc.). Chassis
no. 46 482.

Links/à gauche/left:
Bugatti T. 46 Roadster 1930
(ohne Ersatzräder/sans roues
de secours/without spare
wheels). Chassis no. 46 125.

Bugatti T. 46 Berline 1935
(Milion-Guiet, Patent de Vis-
caya, Aluminium). Chassis no.
46 523.

Oben/en haut/above: Bugatti T. 46 Chassis.

Rechts/à droite/right: Bugatti T. 47 Chassis, entwickelt für die 24 Stunden von Le Mans/ construite pour les 24 heures du Mans/developed for the Le Mans 24 hour race, 1929 (16 cyl., 60 x 66 mm, 2986 cc.). Chassis no. 47 155.

Rechts/à droite/right:
Bugatti T. 46 Chassis mit
Drahtspeichenrädern/à
roues fil/with wire
wheels.

Links/à gauche/left:
Bugatti-Motor T. 49 (8 cyl., 72 x 100 mm, 3257 cc.,
hier mit Einfachzündung/pourvu ici d'un
allumage simple/here with single ignition).

Oben/ci-dessus/above:
Bugatti T. 46 S Coach 1932
(8 cyl., 81 x 130 mm, 5359 cc.,
mit Kompressor/à compres-
seur/with supercharger).

Rechts/à droite/right:
Bugatti T. 49 Berline 1932–34
(8 cyl., 72 x 100 mm, 3257 cc.).
Chassis no. 49 414.

Von oben/de haut en bas/from above:
Bugatti T. 49 Cabriolet (Gangloff?) 1931–32 (8 cyl., 72 x 100 mm, 3257 cc.). Chassis no. 49 172;
Bugatti T. 49 Cabriolet (wahrscheinlich Schweizer Karosserie/probablement carrossé en Suisse/probably Swiss body); Chassis no. 49 445.

Von oben/de haut en bas/from above:
Bugatti T. 49 Berline 1933–34; Chassis no. 49 414;
Bugatti T. 49 Cabriolet (Chassis T. 44), 1930 (8 cyl., 72 x 100 mm, 3257 cc.). Chassis no. 44 918.

Bugatti T. 46 Roadster, ca. 1935, Chassis no. 46 287.

Rechts/à droite/right:
Bugatti T. 49 Coupé (Gangloff?), ca. 1932, Chassis no.
49 210.

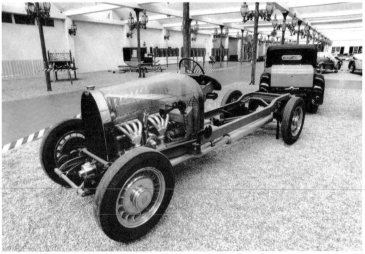

Oben/ci-dessus/above:
Bugatti T. 49 Coupé 1934,
Chassis no. 49 471.

Oben/ci-dessus/above:
Bugatti T. 46, Chassis no.
49 368.

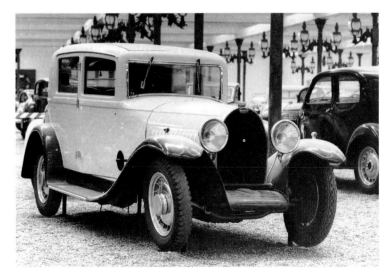

Bugatti T. 49 Berline 1931/32
(ohne Ersatzräder/sans roues
de secours/without spare
wheels), Chassis no. 49 315.

Links: Bugatti T. 49 Limousine, einem T. 46 sehr ähnlich. Der Kühler stammt vom T. 57 (8 cyl., 72 x 100 mm, 3257 cc.), Chassis no. 49 564.

A gauche, une Bugatti T. 49 Berline, carrossée comme une T. 46. Le radiateur provient d'un type 57 (8 cyl., 72 x 100 mm, 3257 cc.), châssis no. 49 564.

Left, a Bugatti T. 49 saloon, looking very much like a T. 46. The radiator came from a T. 57 (8 cyl., 72 x 100 mm, 3257 cc.), chassis no. 49 564.

Oben links/ci-dessus, à gauche/above, left:
Motor/moteur/engine T. 49
oben/ci-dessus/above:
Bugatti T. 49 Coupé Gangloff 1934 (8 cyl., 72 x 100 mm, 3257 cc.). Chassis no. 49 501.

Links/à gauche/left:
Bugatti T. 49 Coach (Van Vooren) Ventoux 1934, Chassis no. 49 559.

Links/à gauche/left:
Bugatti T. 50 Chassis 1930–33
(8 cyl., 86 x 107 mm, 4972 cc.,
2 ohc, mit Kompressor/à
compresseur/with supercharger).

Rechts/à droite/right:
Achtzylinder-Dampfmotor, in
den dreißiger Jahren von
Ettore Bugatti für eine Loko-
motive seiner Konstruktion
entworfen/moteur à vapeur
8 cylindres, construit par Ettore
Bugatti pour une locomotive
dessinée par lui-même dans les
années trente/8 cylinder steam
engine built by Ettore Bugatti
for a locomotive designed by
himself in the thirties.

Unten/ci-dessous/below:
Bugatti T. 50 Cabriolet 1935
(8 cyl., 86 x 107 mm, 4972 cc.,
2 ohc, mit Kompressor/ à
compresseur/with supercharger). Chassis no. 50 160.

Links/à gauche/left:
Bugatti T. 51 Grand Prix 1932–
34 (8 cyl., 60 x 100 mm, 2262
cc., 2 ohc, mit Kompressor/
à compresseur/with super-
charger). Räder vom T. 35/
roues d'une T. 35/wheels from
a T. 35.

Oben/ci-dessus/above:
Bugatti T. 50 B Monoposto
1939 (84 x 107 mm, 4739 cc.,
2 ohc, 470 hp, mit Kompressor/
à compresseur/with super-
charger). Sieger/vainqueur/
winner Coupe des Prisonniers
1945 (Wimille); Chassis no.
50 180.

Oben: Bugatti T. 35A, jedoch
viele Merkmale des 35B/mais
beaucoup de détails de la
35B/however, with many
details indicating a 35B.

Rechts/à droite/right:
Bugatti T. 51 Grand Prix 1932–
35 (8 cyl., 60 x 100 mm, 2262
cc., 2 ohc, mit Kompressor/
avec compresseur/with supercharger).

Links/à gauche/left:
Bugatti T. 51A compétition
1.5 l 1933–34 (8 cyl., 60 x 66 mm,
1493 cc., 2 ohc, mit Kompres-
sor/à compresseur/with
supercharger), Chassis no.
51A134A.

Oben/en haut/above:
Bugatti T. 50B compétition
1939 (8 cyl., 86 x 107 mm,
4972 cc., 2 ohc, mit Kompres-
sor/à compresseur/with supercharger), Grand Prix de
Comminges 1939.

Unten/ci-dessous/below:
Seitenansicht des T. 50B wie
oben mit seinen Zwillingsrä-
dern/le profil de la T. 50B,
montrée ci-dessus, avec ses
roues doubles/another view of
the T. 50B shown above with
those twin rear wheels.

Rechts/à droite/
right:
Bugatti-Chassis
T. 53 1931 (ohne
Motor, Vierrad-
antrieb/sans
moteur, à
quatre roues
motrices/with-
out engine,
four wheel
drive).

78 BUGATTI

Rechts/à droite/right:
Bugatti T. 55 Roadster 1933–34
(8 cyl., 60 x 100 mm, 2262 cc., 2 ohc,
mit Kompressor/à compresseur/
with supercharger). Chassis no.
55 215.

Links/à gauche/left:
Bugatti T. 55 Roadster 1933–34.
Chassis no. 55 237.

Rechts/à droite/right:
Bugatti T. 55 Faux-Cabriolet
1933. Chassis no. 55 203.

Oben/en haut/above:
Bugatti T. 55 Roadster 1933–
34 (hier mit Türen und Rä-
dern vom T. 43/ici avec les
portes et les roues d'une T. 43/
here with doors and wheels
from a T. 43). Chassis no.
55 225.

Bugatti T. 55 Faux-Cabriolet
1933–34, ohne Trittbretter/sans
marchepieds/without run-
ning boards. Chassis no. 55 204.

Links/à gauche/left:
Bugatti T. 43 Roadster (Erdmann & Rossi, Berlin) 1930–31 (8 cyl., 60 x 100 mm, 2262 cc., mit Kompressor/à compresseur/with supercharger). Chassis no. 43 198.

Ettore Bugattis Elektrowagen Typ 56, den er zu Fahrten im eigenen Betrieb benutzte/ Voiture électrique T. 56, dont se servait Ettore Bugatti dans l'usine/Ettore Bugatti used this electric vehicle T. 56 in the factory area.

Rechts/à droite/right:
Bugatti T. 55 Coupé, 1933–34,
Chassis no. 55 212.

Links/à gauche/left:
Bugatti T. 57 Coach Ventoux
1935–38 (8 cyl., 72 x 100 mm,
3257 cc., 2 ohc). Chassis no.
57 721.

Rechts/à droite/right:
Bugatti T. 57 Coach Ventoux
1935–36 (8 cyl., 72 x 100 mm,
3257 cc.). Chassis no. 57 356.

Links/à gauche/left:
Bugatti T. 57 Coach Ventoux
mit abgedeckten Hinterrädern/
les roues arrière sont cachées/
with rear wheel covers.
Chassis no. 57496.

Rechts/à droite/right:
Bugatti T. 57 Coach Ventoux
mit Trittbrettern/avec
marchepieds/with running
boards. Chassis no. 57611.

Oben und rechts/ci-dessus et
à droite/above and right:
Bugatti T. 57 Coach (Larbour-
dette) 1936–38. Chassis no.
57457.

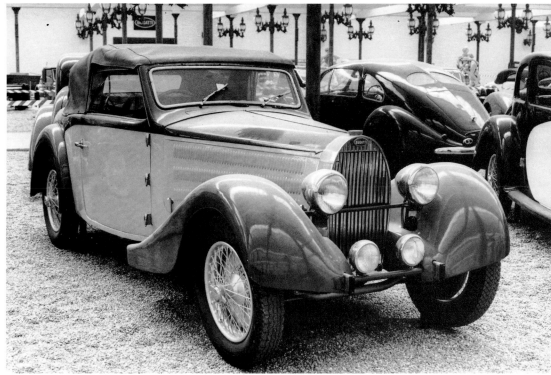

Oben/en haut/above:
Bugatti T. 57C Cabriolet 1938
(8 cyl., 72 x 100 mm, 3257 cc.,
2 ohc, mit Kompressor/à
compresseur/with super-
charger).

Links/à gauche/left:
Bugatti T. 57 Cabriolet (Gangloff), Chassis no. 57 403.

Oben/ci-dessus/above:
Bugatti T. 57 Coach Ventoux
(8 cyl., 72 x 100 mm, 3257 cc.,
2 ohc). Chassis no. 57 616.

Oben/ci-dessus/above:
Bugatti T. 57C Coupé Atalante
(Jean Bugatti/Gangloff) 1937
(8 cyl., 72 x 100 mm, 3257 cc.,
2 ohc, mit Kompressor/à
compresseur/with supercharger). Chassis no. 57C539.

Unten/ci-dessous/below:
Bugatti T. 57 Cabriolet (Gangloff) 1938, Chassis no. 57 764.

Oben rechts/en haut, à droite/
above, right:
Bugatti T. 57 C Berline Galibier
1936–37; Chassis no. 57C636.

Rechts/à droite/right:
Der gleiche Wagen wie oben
links/la même voiture qu'en
haut à gauche/same car as
above, left.

Oben/en haut/above:
Bugatti T. 57 Cabriolet
(Carrosserie Saoutchik, nach
dem Krieg gebaut/construite
après la guerre/post-war coachwork). Chassis no. 57417.

Oben/ci-dessus/above:
Bugatti T. 57C Berline Galibier
1939 (eine der letzten Karosse-
rien von Jean Bugatti/une des
dernières carrosseries dessinées
par Jean Bugatti/one of the last
bodies designed by Jean
Bugatti). Chassis no. 57C789.

Oben/en haut/ above:
Bugatti T. 73C Chassis 1947
(4 cyl., 76 x 82 mm, 1488 cc.,
2 ohc, mit Kompressor/à
compresseur/with supercharger).

Links/à gauche/left:
Bugatti T. 57S Cabriolet
(Vanden Plas) 1937 (8 cyl.,
72 x 100 mm, 3257 cc., 2 ohc).
Chassis no. 57S572.

Rechte Seite oben/page
suivante, en haut/opposite
page, top:
Bugatti T. 57S Cabriolet (Van
Vooren) 1937; Chassis no.
57S571.
Darunter/en bas/below:
Bugatti T. 57SC Coach (Ghia,
karossiert nach dem Krieg/
carrossée après la guerre/post-
war body). Chassis no.
57SC561.

Rechts/à droite/right:
Bugatti T. 57SC (Corsica)
1938 (8 cyl., 72 x 100 mm,
3257 cc., 2 ohc, mit Kom-
pressor/à compresseur/
with supercharger). Chassis
no. 57SC602.

Links/à gauche/left:
Bugatti T. 57S Cabriolet 1937.
Chassis no. 57S543.

Rechts/à droite/right:
Bugatti T. 57S Coupé Atalante
(wahrscheinlich/probablement
/probably Gangloff 1937).
Chassis no. 57S471.

Oben: Beeindruckend die große Reihe schöner Maseratis. Vorn ein 1930 2500 8-Zylinder mit Kompressor, dahinter ein 8CM 1933 und Dr Farinas 4CLT 1500 A von 1948. Links ein Gordini 20 S von 1954.

Les Maserati – quelle magnificence! Au premier plan une 2500 8 cylindres à compresseur de 1930, derrière une 8CM de 1933 et la 4CLT 1500 A du Dr Farinas, de 1948. A gauche, une Gordini 20 S de 1954.

A quite impressive row of Maseratis. In front, a 1930 2500 8-cylinder with supercharger, flanked by a 1933 8CM and Dr Farinas 4CLT 1500 A which was driven by the champion in 1948. Left, one of the fine Gordinis, a 1954 model 20 S.

Links: Eines der ältesten Bugatti-Modelle der Sammlung, ein Typ 13. Darunter die gesamte T35-Familie. Rechts ein Typ 59 Grand Prix de Comminges 1939 mit 50 B-Motor (4,7 Liter), den Wimille letztmalig vor Kriegsausbruch steuerte. Darunter ein Typ 49 Cabriolet, gebaut 1931/32.

A gauche, une des plus vieilles Bugatti, un type 13. Ci-dessous, toute la série T. 35. Page suivante, la type 59 du Grand Prix de Comminges 1939 (piloté par Wimille) à moteur T. 50 B et un Cabriolet T. 49 de 1931/32.

Left, one of the oldest Bugattis in the museum, a type 13. Below, the T. 35 family in the Grand Prix corner...
Opposite page, the T. 59 Comminges Grand Prix car with T. 50B engine (4.7 litres), driven by Wimille in 1939, and a 1931/32 T. 49 cabriolet.

Unten: Der berühmte Bugatti Typ 32, gebaut für den Großen Preis von Frankreich 1923. Daneben einer der zahlreich vertretenen Typ 57S, Typ Atalante.

Ci-dessous, un des quatre «tanks» type 32 engagés dans le Grand Prix de l'ACF en 1923, et un des nombreux modèles 57S, type Atalante.

Below, one of the type 32 Bugatti Tanks, four of which have been built for the French Grand Prix in 1932. Right, one of the many type 57S Atalante in the Schlumpf collection.

Bugatti Typ 41, genannt la Royale – das berühmte Coupé Napoléon gehörte einst Ettore Bugatti persönlich. Dieser 8-Zylinder (12 763 ccm Hubraum, 300 PS bei 2000 U/min) mit der Chassis-Nummer 41 100 dürfte der wertvollste Wagen der ganzen Sammlung sein.

Le type 41, connu sous le nom de Bugatti Royale. Le célèbre Coupé Napoléon a appartenu jadis à E. Bugatti en personne. Cette 8 cylindres est certainement la voiture la plus prestigieuse au monde.

The most valuable car of the Schlumpf collection: the Bugatti type 41 Royale, called coupé Napoléon. This straight-eight (12 763 cc., 200 bhp at 2000 rpm) has got the chassis number 41 100 and belonged once to the Patron personally.

Dieser Mercedes Typ SS von
1930 stammt aus dem Besitz
einer Engländerin, Mrs. Eccles.
Die Werksbezeichnung dieses
Modells lautet 710 (27/160/
200 PS). Dieser Kompressor-
6-Zylinder ist in ganz hervorragendem Zustand.

Cette Mercedes type SS de 1930,
6 cylindres à compresseur, ayant
appartenu à Mme Eccles, portait
l'appellation 710 (27/160/200 PS) –
un exemplaire magnifique.

This 1930 SS type Mercedes was
called the 710 (27/160/200 PS),
once belonging to Mrs. Eccles.
A pretty specimen of this rare
supercharged 6-cylinder sports
car.

Pic-Pic (Piccard-Pictet) 1912. Diese Marke war in der Schweiz zu Hause.

Piccard-Pictet de 1912, appelée Pic-Pic et fabriquée en Suisse.

1912 Piccard-Pictet, called the Pic-Pic, a Swiss make.

Ferrari Formel 2 Modell 500 1952/53. Der Wagen hat die Nummer 5000 184; der 4-Zylinder-Motor von 1985 ccm Hubraum leistet 185 PS. Einer der wenigen 4-Zylinder dieser Marke, die es gab!

Ferrari F.2 type 500, numéro 5000 184, de 1952/53. Une des très rares 4-cylindres construites par Ferrari (1985 cc., 185 ch).

1952/53 formula 2 Ferrari, model 500, car number 5000 184. One of the few 4-cylinders Ferrari ever built (1985 cc., 185 bhp).

Die Gordini- und dahinter die Alfa Romeo-
Parade. Vorn das Chassis des Gordini 32 (Nr. 41),
ein 8-Zylinder mit 2473 ccm Hubraum aus dem
Jahre 1956. Die Karosserie liegt daneben.

La parade des Gordini et Alfa Romeo.
Au premier plan le châssis d'un modèle
Gordini 32 (no. 41), 8 cylindres, 2473 cc.,
de 1956. A côté, la carrosserie.

Here we have the Gordini and Alfa Romeo
parade. In front, the chassis of a 1956
type 32 Gordini (no. 41), a straight-eight
of 2473 cc.; the body has been put alongside.

Links/à gauche/left:
Bugatti T. 57SC Coupé Atalante 1936–37 (8 cyl.,
72 x 100 mm, 3257 cc., 2 ohc, mit Kompressor/
à compresseur/with supercharger), Chassis
no. 57SC441.

Oben/ci-dessus/above:
Bugatti T. 57S Coupé Atalante
1936–37. Chassis no. 57S481.
Daneben/ci-dessus, à droite/
above, right:
Bugatti T. 64 Coach 1939 (letzter
Entwurf Jean Bugattis/la dernière création de Jean Bugatti/
last design of Jean Bugatti;
8 cyl., 84 x 100 mm, 4432 cc.,
2 ohc).

Rechts/à droite/right:
Bugatti T. 57SC Coupé Atalante
(8 cyl., 72 x 100 mm, 3257 cc.,
2 ohc, mit Kompressor/à
compresseur/with supercharger), Chassis no. 57SC451.

Links/à gauche/left:
Bugatti T. 101 Cabriolet (bei
Bugatti gebaut/construit chez
Bugatti/built in the Bugatti
works) 1952 (8 cyl.,
72 x 100 mm, 3257 cc., 2 ohc).
Chassis no. 101 503.

Rechts/à droite/right:
Bugatti T. 101C Coach 1952
(8 cyl., 72 x 100 mm, 3257 cc.,
2 ohc, mit Kompressor/à
compresseur/with super-
charger). Chassis no. 57454.

Unten/ci-dessous/below:
Bugatti T. 252 „Etorette"
Roadster 1956 (4 cyl.,
76 x 82 mm, 1488 cc., 2 ohc).
Chassis no. 299.

Unten/ci-dessous/below:
Bugatti T. 251 Grand Prix
Monoposto 1956 (8 cyl., 76 x
68.5 mm, 2486 cc., 2 ohc).

Oben/en haut/above:
Bugatti T. 251 Chassis 1956.
Dieser Wagen wurde vom
ehem. Alfetta-Konstrukteur
Colombo entworfen/voiture
de formule 1 conçue par
Colombo, ex-constructeur des
Alfetta/this formula 1 car has
been designed by ex-Alfetta
creator Colombo.

Oben/ci-dessus/above:
Bugatti T. 252 Prototyp für
Straßentest/prototype d'essai/
road test prototype 1956–58.

Oben/en haut/above:
Bugatti T. 68 Roadster,
entworfen während des
Krieges/dessiné pendant la
guerre/designed during the
war (4 cyl., 48.5 x 50 mm,
369 cc., 2 ohc, mit Kompressor/
à compresseur/with super-
charger).

Rechts/à droite/right:
Bugatti T. 73A Coach 1947
(4 cyl., 76 x 82 mm, 1488 cc.,
ohc, mit Kompressor/à
compresseur/with super-
charger).

Rechts/à droite/right:
Bugatti T. 101 Chassis 1951
(8 cyl., 72 x 100 mm, 3257 cc.,
2 ohc).

Links/à gauche/left:
Bugatti T. 101 Berline Prototype
1951 (8 cyl., 72 x 100 mm,
3257 cc., 2 ohc).
Chassis no. 101 500.

Unten/ci-dessous/below:
Motor einer Royale T. 41
(Railcar-Serie)/moteur d'une
Royale T. 41, série railcar/
engine of a T. 41 Royale, railcar
series.

Oben/ci-dessus/above:
Fritz Schlumpfs eigener T. 35B
und zwei Kinder-Elektroautos
T. 52/Bugatti T. 35B, la voiture
personnelle de Fritz Schlumpf,
et deux T. 52 électriques pour
enfants/Fritz Schlumpf's own
T. 35B and two T. 52 baby Bugattis.

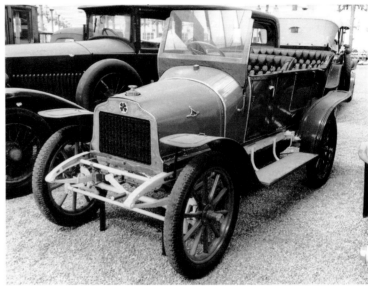

Links/à gauche/left:
Brasier 4 cyl., 1906.

Unten/ci-dessous/below:
Brasier VL Torpedo 1910
(2 cyl., 90 x 120 mm, 1520 cc.,
12 hp/1600).

Rechts/à droite/right:
Charron Double-Phaeton 1910
(4 cyl., 2.4 litre).

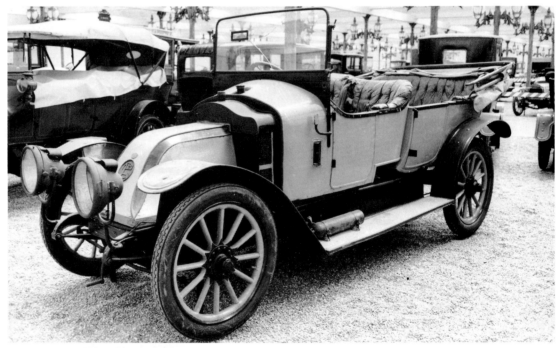

Links/à gauche/left:
B. N. C. Montlhéry Sport 1928
(4 cyl., 60 x 97 mm., 1100 cc.).

Oben/en haut/above:
Cisitalia D. 46 1948
(Fiat 1100, 4 cyl.,
68 x 75 mm, 1086 cc.).

Citroën C3 / 5 CV 1925,
1923, 1924 (4 cyl., 55 x 90 mm,
856 cc.).

Citroën C3 / 5 CV Trèfle 1924
(4 cyl., 55 x 90 mm, 856 cc.).

Clément 1900 (3.5 hp 1 cyl.
Panhard).
Rechts oben/en haut, à droite/
above right:
Clément Voiturette 1900
(2.25 hp 1 cyl. de Dion).

Links/à gauche/left:
Clément-Bayard 4M3 1911
(4 cyl.).

Oben/ci-dessus/above:
Clément-Bayard Torpédo 1913
(2 cyl., 8 hp).

Oben/ci-dessus/above:
Daimler/Coventry Bus 1899
(2 cyl., 6 hp).

Unten/ci-dessous/below:
Daimler/Coventry Straight
Eight Limousine 1936 (8 cyl.,
80 x 115 mm, 4624 cc.).

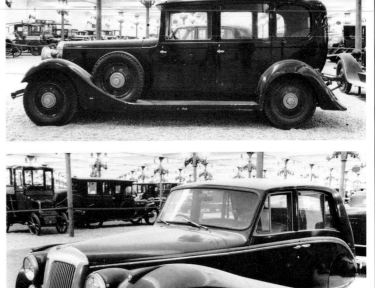

Von oben/de haut en bas/
from above:
Daimler/Coventry 20 HP 1912
(4 cyl., 90 x 130 mm, 3309 cc.,
syst. Knight).
Daimler/Coventry Straight
Eight Hooper Limousine 1938
(8 cyl., 80 x 115 mm, 4624 cc.).
Daimler/Coventry DB 18
Tickford Cabriolet 1939
(6 cyl., 69 x 110 mm, 2522 cc.).

Rechts/à droite/right:
Daimler/Coventry DE 36
Hooper Limousine 1954
(8 cyl., 85 x 120 mm, 5460 cc.).

Oben/en haut/above:
Darracq Tourer 1911 (4 cyl.).

Links/à gauche/left:
Darracq Tonneau 1902 (1 cyl.).

Darracq 20/28 hp Coupé
Chauffeur 1907 (4 cyl., 4700 cc.).

Rechts/à droite/right:
De Dion Tricycle 1897 (1 cyl.,
250 cc., 1¾ hp); darunter ein
Modell 1898/ci-dessous un
modèle de 1898/left, below,
a 1898 model.

Links/à gauche/left:
De Dion-Bouton 6 hp Phaeton
1904 (1 cyl., 90 x 110 mm,
700 cc., 6 hp).

Oben/ci-dessus/above:
De Dion-Bouton 12 hp
Phaeton 1908 (4 cyl.,
75 x 100 mm, automatischer
Vergaser/carburateur
automatique/automatic
carburetor).

Rechts/à droite/right:
De Dion-Bouton 8 hp Double-
Phaeton 1904 (1 cyl.,
100 x 120 mm, 943 cc.,
8 hp/1200).

Links/à gauche/left:
De Dion-Bouton 6 hp 1904
(1 cyl., 90 x 110 mm, 700 cc.).

Oben/ci-dessus/above:
De Dion-Bouton 8 hp 1904
(1 cyl., 100 x 120 mm, 943 cc.,
8 hp/1200).

Rechts/à droite/right:
De Dion-Bouton Tonneau
10 hp 1905 (2 cyl., 80 x 110 mm).

Unten/ci-dessous/below:
De Dion-Bouton-1-Zylinder-
Wagen 1904/05/De Dion-
Bouton monocylindre/De
Dion-Bouton single-cylinder
car.

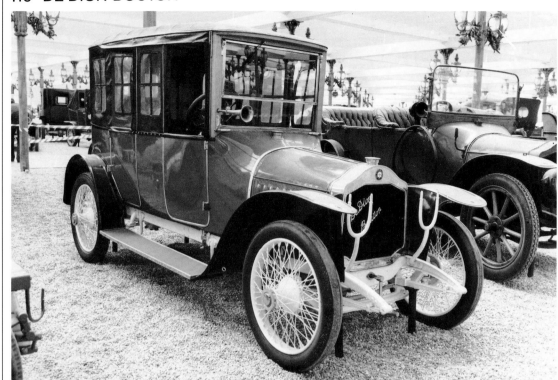

De Dion-Bouton 12/16 hp
Tourer 1914 (4 cyl.,
75 x 130 mm).

Unten/ci-dessous/below:
De Dion-Bouton 6 hp Torpédo
1912 (2 cyl., 66 x 120 mm).

Links/à gauche/left:
De Dion-Bouton 18 hp Torpédo
1911 (4 cyl., 90 x 120 mm).

Oben/en haut/above:
De Dion-Bouton AV 10 hp
1907 (2 cyl., 80 x 120 mm).

Rechts/à droite/right:
De Dion-Bouton 18 hp 1911
(4 cyl., 90 x 110 mm).

Links/à gauche/left:
De Dion-Bouton 1910
Type CF 10 hp Limousine
1910 (4 cyl., 66 x 100 mm).

Unten/ci-dessous/below:
Décauville Tonneau 1904
(2 cyl., 12 hp).

De Dion-Bouton Type DJ
14 HP Torpédo 1913 (4 cyl.,
80 x 140 mm).

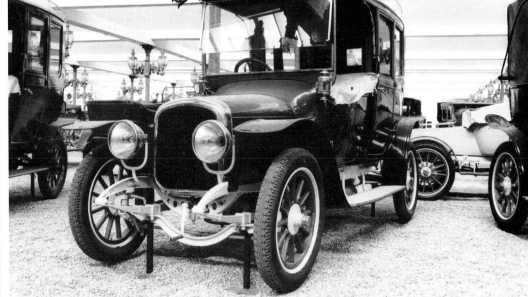

Delahaye 18 CV Torpédo
1912 (6 cyl., 75 x 120 mm,
3170 cc., 24 hp).

Delahaye Coupé Chauffeur
1914 (4 cyl., 4 litres).
Unten/ci-dessous/below:
Delage Double-Phaeton 1907
(4 cyl., 90 x 100 mm, 15 hp de
Dion).

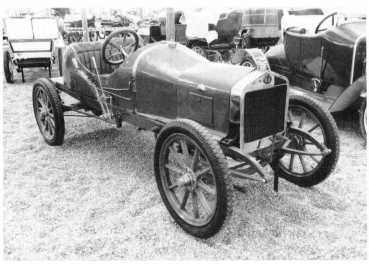

Links/à gauche/left:
Delage 1908 1 cyl. de Dion,
Aufbau nicht original/
carrosserie non d'origine/body
not original.

Oben/ci-dessus/above:
Delahaye 12/16 hp 1909
(2 litres).

Links/à gauche/left:
Delaunay-Belleville Limousine 1907 (4 cyl., 40 hp).

Unten/ci-dessous/below:
Delaunay-Belleville 1912 (6 cyl.).

Rechts/à droite/right:
Fouillaron Tonneau
1902 (2 cyl., 12 hp).

Links/à gauche/left:
Dufaux Gordon-Bennett
70/90 hp 1904 (8 cyl., 12 763 cc.).

Oben/ci-dessus/above:
Farman A6B 1927 (6 cyl.,
6600 cc.).

Oben/ci-dessus/above:
Esculape 1899 (1 cyl. de Dion
2.25 hp).

Farman A6B 1925 (6 cyl.,
6600 cc.).

Links/à gauche/left:
Ferrari F.2 Type 500 1952/53
(4 cyl., 90 x 78 mm, 1984 cc.,
170–200 hp).

Links unten/en bas, à gauche/
below, left:
Ferrari F.1 Type 158 1953
(V6, 67 x 52.8 mm, 1489 cc.,
200 hp/10 500); John Surtees
Champion GP Deutschland
1963.

Oben/en haut/above:
Ferrari F.2 Type 125 1950/51
(V12, 55 x 52.2 mm, 1498 cc.,
118 hp/6500), gefahren von/
pilotée par/driven by Villoresi,
Ascari etc.

Ferrari F.2 Type 166 1949
(V12, 60 x 58.8 mm, 1995 cc.,
160 hp/7000), Karosserie stark
verändert/carrosserie modifiée/
body modified.

Oben links/en haut à gauche/above, left:
Ferrari F.2 Type 500 1952 (4 cyl., 90 x 78 mm, 1984 cc., 180 hp/7000).

Links/à gauche/left:
Ferrari Spider California Type 250 GT 1962 (V12, 73 x 58.8 mm, 2953 cc., 240 hp/7000).

Oben/en haut/above:
Ferrari Testa Rossa Type 500 1956 (4 cyl., 90 x 78 mm, 1985 cc., 180 hp/7000).

Rechts/à droite/right:
Ferrari Type 250 GT Tour de France (Pininfarina/Scaglietti) 1957/58 (V12, 73 x 58.8 mm, 2953 cc., 300 hp/7200).

Oben/ci-dessus/above:
Ferrari Type 250 LM 1964 (V12, 73 x 58,8 mm, 2953 cc., 300 hp/7500), als GT nicht homologiert/non homologué comme GT/not homologated as GT.

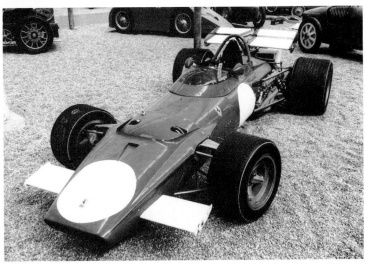

Oben/ci-dessus/above:
Ferrari F.1 Type 312 B 1971 (F 12, 78.5 x 51.5 mm, 2991 cc., 480 hp/11 500), gefahren von Ickx und Regazzoni/pilotée par Ickx et Regazzoni/driven by Ickx and Regazzoni.

Fiat 508 Balilla Sport 1934
(4 cyl., 65 x 75 mm, 995 cc.,
36 hp/4400).

Fiat 509 Cabriolet 1925 (4 cyl.,
57 x 97 mm, 990 cc.,
22 hp/3400).

Links/à gauche/left:
Georges Richard 6 hp 1900
(2 cyl.), caross. Vedrine.

Unten/ci-dessous/below:
Georges Richard Victoria
1894 (1 cyl., 130 x 150 mm,
2000 cc., Benz).

Rechts/à droite/right:
Georges Richard 7,5 hp 1901
(2 cyl.) Tonneau.

Links/à gauche/left:
Le Gui Phaeton 1911 (4 cyl., 15 hp).

Rechts/à droite/right:
Grégoire 12 hp 1907 (2 cyl.).

Links/à gauche/left:
Gladiator 20 hp 1907 (4 cyl.).

Rechts/à droite/right:
Simca-Gordini Sport 1939
(4 cyl., 76 x 75 mm, 1100 cc.),
Klassensiege/victorieuse dans sa
catégorie/class wins: 24 h
du Mans 1939, Grand Prix de
Reims 1939, Côte de la Turbie
1939, Grand Prix de Com-
minges 1939, Bois de
Boulogne 1945 etc.

Links/à gauche/left:
Simca-Gordini Sport 1937
(4 cyl., 52 x 67 mm, 569 cc.,
»Simca Cinq«), Sieger/vain-
queur/winner Index Per-
formance Le Mans 1937.

Rechts/à droite/right:
Gordini F.1 1954 (6cyl.,
80 x 82 mm, 2473 cc., 220 hp/
6000).

Rechts/à droite/right:
Gordini »Le Mans« 1951
(4 cyl., 78 x 78 mm, 1491 cc.,
mit Kompressor/à com-
presseur/with supercharger).

Unten/ci-dessous/below:
Gordini 20 S Sport 1954
(6 cyl., 1987 cc.).

Links/à gauche/left:
Derselbe Wagen wie auf Seite 120 unten/
la même voiture qu'à la page 120, en
bas/same car as on page 120, bottom).

Oben/en haut/above:
Gordini 20 S Roadster 1954
(6 cyl., 1987 cc.).

Gordini Grand Prix Type 32
Chassis no. 41, 1956 (8 cyl.,
2 ohc, 2473 cc.). Die Ka-
rosserie liegt neben dem

Wagen/à côté, la carrosserie/
the body is beside the car.

Links/à gauche/left:
Gordini Type 26 S Sport 1952
(6 cyl., 2300 cc.).

Unten/ci-dessous/below:
Gordini Type 24 S Sport 1956
(6 cyl., 2982 cc.).

Links/à gauche/left:
Gordini Werksprototyp/proto-
type d'usine/work's prototype 1954.

Oben/en haut/above:
Gordini Type 17S Roadster
1952 (4 cyl., 1500 cc.).

Oben/ci-dessus/above:
Gordini Type 23 S Montlhéry
1956 (6 cyl., 2982 cc.).

Gordini Grand Prix
Type 32 1956 (8 cyl., 2473 cc.)
Dieser Wagen Nr. 42 war der
letzte Gordini-Rennwagen/
cette voiture N° 42 fut
la dernière Gordini de
course/this formula 1 car
bearing the number 42 was
the last Gordini competition
car.

Die gesamte Gordini-Kollek-
tion im Museum erhielt
Schlumpf von Amédée
Gordini, als dieser den Bau
eigener Wagen aufgab und zu
Simca ging.
Toutes les Gordini du musée
ont été données à Schlumpf
par Amédée Gordini lorsque
il est passé chez Simca après
avoir cessé de construire pour
son compte.
The whole collection of
Gordinis is a gift of Amédée
Gordini when he retired from
producing own cars, taking
over a position with Simca.

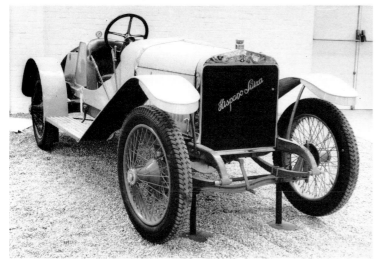

Oben links/en haut à gauche/above, left:
Hispano-Suiza Alfonso XIII Compétition 1912 (4 cyl., 80 x 180 mm, 3620 cc., 64 hp/2300).

Oben rechts/en haut à droite/above, right: Hispano-Suiza Chassis Type VII 1914 (4 cyl., sv, 4700 cc.).

Links/à gauche/left:
Hispano-Suiza 54 CV (Vanvooren) Type 68, 1931 (12 cyl., 100 x 100 mm, 9424 cc., 210 hp/2400).

Unten/ci-dessous/below:
Hispano-Suiza 46 CV Coupé Type H6B, 1930 (6 cyl., 110 x 140 mm, 7983 cc., ohc, 140 hp).

Hispano-Suiza K-6 Coupé de Maître 1935 (6 cyl., 100 x 110 mm, 5148 cc., ohv, 140 hp/3500).

Hispano-Suiza 54 CV Type 68
Coupé Chauffeur 1931 (12 cyl.,
100 x 100 mm, 9424 cc.,
210 hp/2400).

Oben/ci-dessus/above:
Hispano-Suiza 54 CV Type 68
Cabriolet 1932 (12 cyl.,
100 x 100 mm, 9424 cc.,
210 hp/2400).

Oben/ci-dessus/above:
Horch 830 Cabriolet 1933 (V8,
75 x 85 mm, 3004 cc.,
62 hp/3200).

Oben/ci-dessus/above:
Horch 670 Cabriolet 1932
(12 cyl., 80 x 100 mm, 6021 cc.,
120 hp/3200).

Links/à gauche/left:
Horch 450 Cabriolet 1931
(8 cyl., 87 x 95 mm, 4517 cc.,
ohc, 90 hp/3400).

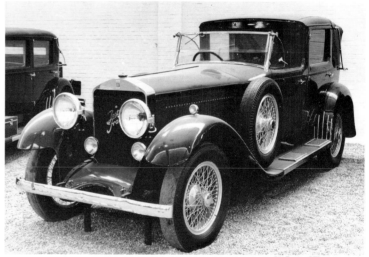

Links/à gauche/left:
Isotta-Fraschini Tipo 8A
Limousine 1928.

Von oben/de haut en bas/
from above:
Isotta-Fraschini Tipo 8A
(Carosserie Cesare Sala,
Milano) 1930 (8 cyl., 93 x
130 mm, 7372 cc., 120 hp/2400);
Isotta-Fraschini Tipo 8A
Sedanca/Landaulet, 1929.

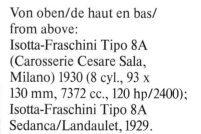

Links/à gauche/left:
Hurtu dos-à-dos 3 hp 1897
(1 cyl., 130 x 150 mm,
2000 cc., Benz);
Hurtu Torpedo 1907 (2 cyl.,
Aster).

Jacquot Dampfwagen/voiture à vapeur/steam car 1876.

Rechts oben/en haut à droite/ above, right:
La Licorne Voiturette 1908 (2 cyl. de Dion).

Rechts/à droite/right:
Léon Bollée Tricar 1896 (1 cyl., 650 cc.).

Links/à gauche/left:
Lancia Lambda, 8. ser. Lungo 1928 (4 cyl., 82 x 120 mm, 2570 cc., 69 hp/3500).

Unten links/ci-dessous à gauche/below, left:
Lancia Dilambda Touring 1929 (8 cyl., 79 x 100 mm, 3960 cc., 100 hp/3800)

Unten/ci-dessous/below:
Lancia Epsilon Torpedo 1913 (4 cyl., 100 x 130 mm, 4080 cc.).

Lorraine-Dietrich 40 CV 1914
Torpédo (4 cyl., 125 x 170 mm,
8340 cc.).

Links/à gauche/left:
Lorraine-Dietrich 12 CV
Coach 1911 (4 cyl., 2121 cc.).

Lorraine-Dietrich 1911 (4 cyl.)
Feuerwehrwagen/voiture de
pompiers/fire engine.

Rechts/à droite/right:
Lorraine-Dietrich 16 CV
Coupé Chauffeur-Landaulet
1913 (4 cyl.).

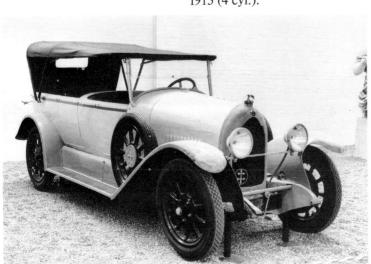

Links/à gauche/left:
Lorraine-Dietrich 15 CV
Torpédo 1926 (6 cyl., 75 x
130 mm, 3446 cc., 50 hp/2100).

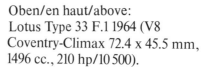

Oben/en haut/above:
Lotus Type 33 F.1 1964 (V8
Coventry-Climax 72.4 x 45.5 mm,
1496 cc., 210 hp/10 500).

Oben/ci-dessus/above:
Lotus Type 18 F.1 1960/61 (4 cyl.,
94 x 90 mm, 2495 cc., 239 hp/
6750), lief mit verschiedenen
Motoren 1 Liter u. 1,5 Liter/cette
voiture fut équipée de
moteurs 1 et 1.5 litre/this
model was raced with various
engine types, also 1 and 1.5 litre.

Lotus Grand Prix Type
Mk. 24, 1962–63 (4 cyl., 81,8 x
71,1 mm, 1496 cc.,
155 hp/7500, Coventry Climax).

Links/à gauche/left:
Mathis SB 1923 (4 cyl.,
60 x 100 mm, 1131 cc.).

Oben/ci-dessus/above:
MAF (Markranstadter Auto-
mobil-Fabrik) 5/14 PS 1914
(4 cyl., 68 x 90 mm, 1375 cc.,
14 hp/2200); Chassis no. 890.

Oben/en haut/above:
Maserati 8C-2500 1934 (8 cyl.,
65 x 94 mm, 2 ohc, 2495 cc.,
175 hp/6000 mit Kompressor/
à compresseur/with super-
charger).

Rechts/à droite/right:
Maserati 4CL Monoposto
‚Voiturette‘ 1939 (78 x 78 mm,
1498 cc., 220 hp/6600 mit
Kompressor/à com-
presseur/with supercharger);
eingesetzt bis 1949. Front nicht
original/engagée jusqu'en 1949,
prise d'air du radiateur non
d'origine/raced until 1949,
radiator grill not original.

Maserati 8 CM 1934 (8 cyl.,
69 x 100 mm, 2 ohc, 2992 cc.,
210 hp/5600 mit Kompressor/
à compresseur/with super-
charger).

Rechts/à droite/right:
Maserati 4 CLT 1500 A compressore 1948 (4 cyl., 78 x
78 mm, 1490 cc., 260 hp/7000);
ex-Dr. Farina.

Oben/en haut/above:
Maserati 250 F, Version 1957
(6 cyl., 84 x 72 mm, 2493 cc.,
240 hp/6500).

Oben rechts/en haut à droite/
above, right:
Maserati A6SSG F.2 1953
(6 cyl., 76.2 x 72 mm, 1988 cc.,
190 hp/8000).

Rechts/à droite/right:
Maserati 250 F 1958 (V12,
68.7 x 56 mm, 2490 cc.,
310 hp/10 000).

Maserati 250 F Grand Prix
1954/55 (6 cyl., 84 x 72 mm,
2493 cc., 240 hp/6500).

Unten/ci-dessous/below:
Maurer Union, Nürnberg Type 1, 1901
(1 cyl., 110 x 120 mm, 1140 cc., 5 hp/800);
wahrscheinlich eines der ersten Exemplare/
probablement un des premiers modèles/
probably one of the first Maurer cars.

Oben/en haut/above:
Maybach Zeppelin (Spohn)
Landaulet 1929 (12 cyl., 92 x
100 mm, 7977 cc., 200 hp/
3000); Chassis no. 1277.

Rechts/à droite/right:
Maybach Zeppelin DS8
(Spohn) Limousine 1930
(12 cyl., 92 x 100 mm, 7977 cc.,
220 hp/3000) ex D. Busch,
Lüdenscheid; Chassis no. 1317.

Links/à gauche/left:
Maybach SW 38 Limousine
1937 (6 cyl., 90 x 100 mm,
3790 cc., ohc, 140 hp/4000);
Chassis no. 1820.

Oben/ci-dessus/above:
Maybach SW 38 Cabriolet
(Erdmann & Rossi) 1937;
Chassis no. 1800.

Oben/en haut/above:
Maybach Zeppelin Cabriolet (Graber) 1934 (12 cyl., 92 x 100 mm, 7977 cc., 200 hp/ 3000).

Links/à gauche/left:
Maybach SW 38 Pullman Limousine (Spohn) 1937 (6 cyl., 90 x 100 mm, 3790 cc., ohc, 140 hp/4000); Chassis no. 1721.

Unten links/ci-dessous à gauche/below, left:
Minerva AN 12 CV Limousine 1928 (6 cyl., 68 x 92 mm, 2004 cc.)

Rechts/à droite/right:
Minerva 20 CV Grand Sport Torpédo 1928 (6 cyl., 80 x 112 mm, 3400 cc.).

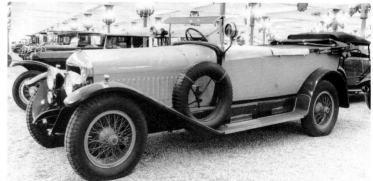

Mercedes Simplex 28/32 PS
Phaeton 1905 (4 cyl., 110 x
140 mm, 5320 cc., 33 hp/1200).

Rechts/à droite/right:
Mercedes Sport 39/75 PS 1907
(6 cyl., 120 x 150 mm, 10 178 cc.,
100 hp/1500).

Links/à gauche/left:
Mercedes 14/30 PS Limousine 1910
(4 cyl., 90 x 140 mm, 3564 cc.,
35 hp/1500).

Oben/ci-dessus/above:
Mercedes 6/25/40 PS Targa Florio
Chassis 1923 (4 cyl., 65 x 113 mm,
1499 cc., 2 ohc, Kompressor/
compresseur/supercharger).

Mercedes 400 15/70/100 PS
Tourer 1925 (6 cyl., 80 x
130 mm, 3920 cc., ohc,
Kompressor/compresseur/
supercharger).

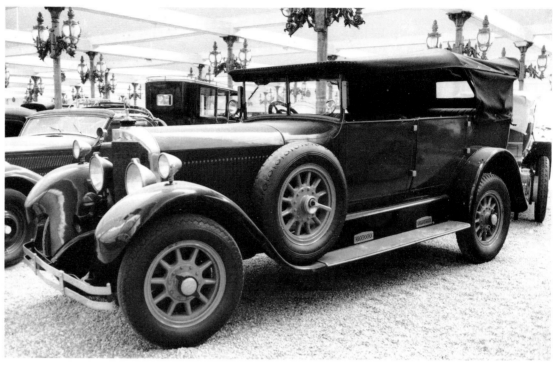

Unten/ci-dessous/below:
Mercedes 28/95 PS Tourer
1923 (6 cyl., 105 x 140 mm,
7250 cc., ohc, Kompressor/
compresseur/supercharger).

Gegenüberliegende Seite oben: Mercedes K 24/110/160 PS Landaulet 1926, unvollständig (6 cyl., 94 x 150 mm, 6240 cc., ohc, Kompressor), darunter Mercedes 600 24/100/140 PS Roadster 1925 (6 cyl., 94 x 150 mm, 6240 cc., Kompressor).

Page suivante: en haut Mercedes K 24/110/160 PS landaulet, 1926, incomplète (6 cyl., 94 x 150 mm, 6240 cc., ohc, compresseur); en dessous Mercedes 600 24/110/140 PS roadster 1925 (6 cyl., 94 x 150 mm, 6240 cc., compresseur).

Opposite page, 1926 Mercedes K 24/110/160 PS landaulet, incomplete (6 cyl., 94 x 150 mm, 6240 cc., ohc, supercharger); below 1925 Mercedes 600 24/110/140 PS roadster (6 cyl., 94 x 150 mm, 6240 cc., supercharger).

Linke Seite/Page de gauche/
left page: Mercedes-Benz SS 1930
(Type 710) 27/160/200 PS, 1930,
(6 cyl., 100 x 150 mm, 7065 cc.,
ohc, Kompressor/compres-
seur/supercharger)

Mercedes-Benz SSK (Type 720)
27/170/225 PS, 1929 (6 cyl.,
100 x 150 mm, 7065 cc., ohc,
Kompressor/compresseur/
supercharger).

Rechts/à droite/right:
Mercedes-Benz SSK (Type
720) 1928; Chassis no. 36372

Unten/ci-dessous/below:
Mercedes-Benz SS (Type 710)
27/160/200 PS Torpédo
(Saoutchik Paris) 1928 (6 cyl.,
100 x 150 mm, 7065 cc., ohc,
Kompressor/compresseur/
supercharger).

Oben links/en haut à gauche/
above, left:
Mercedes-Benz 500 K Chassis
1934 (8 cyl., 86 x 108 mm,
5019 cc., 160 hp/3400 mit
Kompressor/à com-
presseur/with supercharger).

Oben/en haut à droite/above:
Mercedes-Benz 380 Cabriolet
1934 (8 cyl., 78 x 100 mm,
3820 cc., 120 hp/3400 mit
Kompressor/à com-
presseur/with supercharger).

Oben/ci-dessus/above:
Mercedes-Benz 500 K
Roadster 1934 (8 cyl., 86 x
108 mm, 5019 cc., 160 hp/3400
mit Kompressor/à com-
presseur/with supercharger).

Links/à gauche/left:
Mercedes-Benz 540 K
Cabriolet A 1937 (8 cyl.,
88 x 111 mm, 5401 cc., 180 hp/
3400 mit Kompressor/à
compresseur/with super-
charger).

Oben/en haut/above:
Mercedes-Benz 540 K
Cabriolet B 1936; Chassis
no. 130904.

Oben/en haut/above:
Mercedes-Benz 540 K
Cabriolet (Erdmann & Rossi,
Berlin) 1938 (8 cyl., 88 x
111 mm, 5401 cc., 180 hp/3400
mit Kompressor/à com-
presseur/with supercharger).

Mercedes-Benz 770 »Grosser
Mercedes«, Chassis 1938
(8 cyl., 95 x 135 mm, 7655 cc.,
230 hp/3600 mit Kompressor/
à compresseur/with
supercharger).

Mercedes-Benz 7,7 »Grosser Mercedes« Cabriolet D 1938 (8 cyl., 95 x 135 mm, 7655 cc., 230 hp/3600 mit Kompressor/ à compresseur/with super- charger).

Unten/ci-dessous/below: Mercedes-Benz 320 Cabriolet A 1937 (6 cyl., 82.5 x 100 mm, 3207 cc., 78 hp/3150) mit Stoß- stange eines Citroën 15 CV/ avec le pare-chocs d'une Citroën 15 CV/with Citroën 15 CV bumper.

Links/à gauche/left: Mercedes-Benz 320 Cabriolet A 1937 (kurzes Chassis/ châssis court/short wheel- base).

Unten/ci-dessous/below: Mercedes-Benz 170 V Cabrio- let A 1936 (4 cyl., 73.5 x 100 mm, 1697 cc., 38 hp/3400).

Rechts/à droite/right:
Mercedes-Benz 170 H Cabrio-
Limousine 1936 (4 cyl.,
73.5 x 100 mm, 1697 cc.,
38 hp/3400); Räder nicht ori-
ginal/roues non d'origine/
wheels not original.

Mercedes-Benz 300 S
Roadster-Cabriolet A 1955
(6 cyl., 85 x 88 mm, 2996 cc.,
150 hp/5000).

Oben/en haut/above:
Mercedes-Benz 300 Sc Coupé
1955 (6 cyl., 85 x 88 mm,
2996 cc., 175 hp/4500; Ein-
spritzmotor/à injection/fuel
injection).

Unten/ci-dessous/below:
Mercedes-Benz 300 SL Coupé
Flügeltürer/papillon/gullwing
1956 (6 cyl., 85 x 88 mm,
2996 cc., 215/5800, Einspritz-

motor/à injection/fuel injection). Von August 1954 bis
Mai 1957 wurden 1400 Exemplare dieses Modells gebaut/
d'août 1954 à mai 1957,

1400 exemplaires furent
assemblés/from August
1954 to May 1957, 1400 gullwing
coupés have been built.

Links/à gauche/left:
Mercedes-Benz W 154/II
Grand Prix 1939 (Mot.
M 163 K, 12 cyl., 67 x 70 mm,
2962 cc., 480 hp/8200 mit
Kompressor/à com-
presseur/with supercharger).

Unten links/en bas
à gauche/below, left:
Mercedes-Benz W 125 Grand
Prix 1937 (Mot. M 125, V8,
94 x 102 mm, 5660 cc.,
556 hp/5800).

Rechts und unten/à droite et
ci-dessous/right and below:
Mercedes-Benz W 154/II
Grand Prix 1939 (ein zweites
Exemplar/un deuxième
exemplaire/a second one.

Unten/ci-dessous/below:
Mercedes-Benz 300 SLR
Le Mans 1955 (Mot. W 196-S,
V8, 78 x 78 mm, 2982 cc.,
300 hp/7500). Angeblich ist
der Wagen eine Leihgabe von
Daimler-Benz/On dit que
cette voiture a été prêtée
par Daimler-Benz/
The car is said to be on loan
by Messrs Daimler-Benz.

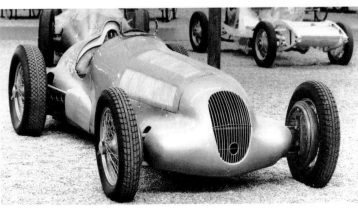

Oben links/en haut à gauche/
above, left:
Monet & Goyon Cyclecar VM
1924 (1 cyl., 350 cc., Villiers).

Oben/en haut à droite/above:
Mors Phaeton Décapotable
1912 (4 cyl., 2500 cc.).

Links/à gauche/left:
Ménier Dampfwagen/véhicule
à vapeur/steam car 1895.

Links/à gauche/left:
Mors SSS Torpédo 1923 (4 cyl.,
2000 cc., Minerva-Knight
20 hp).

Oben/ci-dessus/above:
Monet & Goyon Cyclecar VM
1925 (1 cyl., 350 cc., Villiers).

Links/à gauche/left:
OM (Officine Meccaniche)
2.2 litre Roadster 1931 (6 cyl.,
67 x 100 mm, 2243 cc.,
55 hp/4000).

Rechts/à droite/right:
Panhard-Levassor 1893 (1 cyl.,
130 x 130 mm, 1725 cc., 3 hp).

Links/à gauche/left:
Frontansicht des Pan-
hard-Levassor wie
oben/la même Panhard-
Levassor que ci-dessus
vue de face/
front view of the same
Panhard-Levassor
shown above.

Links/à gauche/left:
Panhard-Levassor
Tonneau 1901 (4 cyl.,
3100 cc., Kettenantrieb/
transmission par chaînes/
chain drive).

Links außen/à l'extrême gauche/far left: Panhard-Levassor geschlossenes Tonneau/coupé tonneau/closed coupé tonneau »Bohème« 1900 (2 cyl.).

Links/à gauche/left: Panhard-Levassor Landaulet Pantz 1899 (2 cyl.).

Unten: der gleiche Panhard-Levassor wie oben links/ci-dessous: la même voiture qu'en haut à gauche/below, the same Panhard-Levassor as above, left.

Rechts/à droite/right: Panhard-Levassor Tonneau 1903 (2 cyl.).

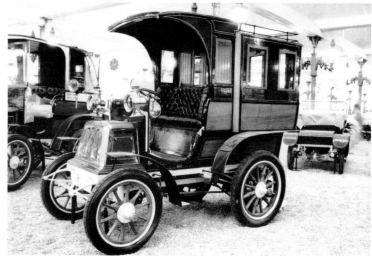

Links/à gauche/left: Panhard-Levassor Course Gordon-Bennett 1905 (4 cyl., 170 x 170 mm, 15 435 cc., 120 hp/1200).

Oben/ci-dessus/above: Panhard-Levassor 12/16 CV Coupé Chauffeur 1909 (4 cyl., 2400 cc.).

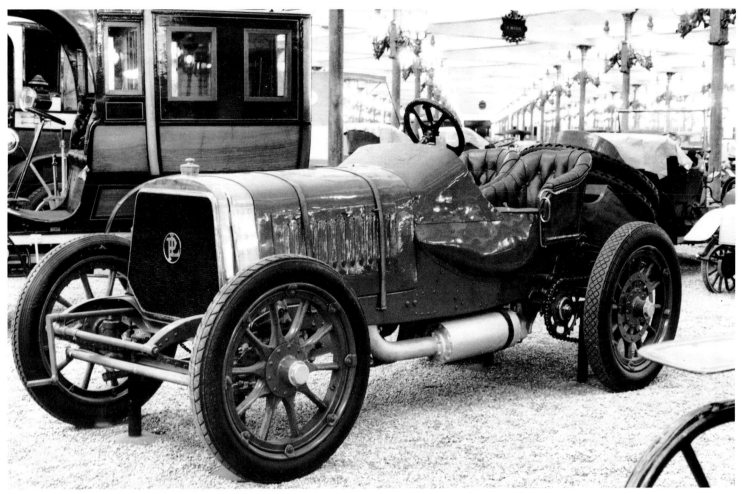

Der gleiche Wagen wie auf der gegenüberliegenden Seite unten links. Bei den Gordon-Bennett-Ausscheidungs-Läufen 1905 in der Auvergne wurde er mit Heath am Steuer Sechster.

La même voiture qu'à la page 148 (en bas à gauche). Pilotée par Heath, cette Panhard arriva 6e de la série éliminatoire sur le circuit d'Auvergne en 1905.

Same car as on opposite page, bottom left. Driven by Heath, this car finished 6th overall in the French Gordon Bennett elimination trials on the Auvergne Circuit in 1905.

Links/à gauche/left:
Panhard-Levassor 25 CV
Limousine 1911 (4 cyl.,
4400 cc.).

Oben/ci-dessus/above:
Pic-Pic (Piccard-Pictet) 12 CV
Limousine 1912 (4 cyl., 83 x
120 mm).

Oben/ci-dessus/above:
Panhard-Levassor 6 litre Limousine 1909 (4 cyl.).

Rechts/à droite/right:
Panhard-Levassor Skiff Tor-
pédo 1920 (4 cyl., 4800 cc.,
Knight).

Rechts/à droite/right:
Panhard-Levassor Limousine
1914 (4 cyl., 7400 cc.). Einst
Wagen des französischen
Präsidenten Poincaré/voiture
du Président Poincaré/once
owned by President Poincaré.

Rechts/à droite/right:
Piccolo 5 PS Voiturette 1906
(2 cyl., 85 x 80 mm, 704 cc.,
5 hp/1300, Kardan/cardan/
shaft drive).

Links/à gauche/left:
Piccolo 7 PS Coupé 1908
(2 cyl., 75 x 90 mm, 794 cc.,
7 hp/1300, Kardan/cardan/
shaft drive).

Unten/ci-dessous/below:
Philos 8 CV Sport 1913 (4 cyl.,
1131 cc., Ballot).

Oben/ci-dessus/above:
Piccolo 5 PS Voiturette 1907
(2 cyl., 75 x 80 mm, 704 cc.,
5 hp/1300, Kardan/cardan/
shaft drive).

Pegaso 102 BS Coupé
(Carrozzeria Touring Milano)
1954 (V8, 75 x 70 mm, 2472 cc.,
2 ohc, 210 hp), unrestauriert/
non restauré/not restored.

Links/à gauche/left:
Peugeot vis-à-vis 1890 (2 cyl.,
1235 cc., 2,5 hp/750, Daimler).

Unten/ci-dessous/below:
Peugeot Type 3 1892 (2 cyl.,
72 x 125 mm, 1018 cc., 3.3 hp).

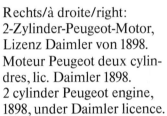

Oben/ci-dessus/above:
Peugeot 8 CV 1901 (2 cyl.,
1056 cc.).

Rechts/à droite/right:
2-Zylinder-Peugeot-Motor,
Lizenz Daimler von 1898.
Moteur Peugeot deux cylindres, lic. Daimler 1898.
2 cylinder Peugeot engine,
1898, under Daimler licence.

Oben/en haut/above:
Peugeot vis-à-vis 12 CV 1892
(2 cyl., 85 x 145 mm, 1645 cc.).

Unten/ci-dessous/below:
Peugeot Fiacre 1897 6 CV
(2 cyl.).

Oben/en haut/above:
Peugeot Type 67 (Châssis allongé) Phaeton 1905
(2 cyl., 105 x 105 mm, 1817 cc., Kettenantrieb/
transmission par chaînes/chain drive model).

Rechts/à droite/right:
Peugeot Torpédo Type 58, 1903 (1 cyl., 102 x
102 mm, 833 cc.).

Peugeot Type 58 Tonneau 1902
(1 cyl., 102 x 102 mm, 833 cc.).

Unten/ci-dessous/below:
Peugeot Type 58 Châssis 1903.

In jenen Jahren gab es bei
Peugeot die unterschiedlich-
sten Kühlerformen.

A cette époque, les formes de
radiateur chez Peugeot
étaient très variées.

In those days, Peugeot
changed shapes of radiator and
bonnet more than once!

Links/à gauche/left:
Peugeot 9 CV Type 65 Voiturette 1904 (2 cyl., 105 x 105 mm, 1817 cc.), ohne Reifen/sans pneus/without tyres.

Rechts/à droite/right:
Peugeot Quadricycle 1905 (1 cyl., 510 cc., 7 hp).

Unten/ci-dessous/below:
Peugeot Type 153 Torpédo 1914 (4 cyl., 80 x 130 mm, 2614 cc.).

Oben: eine Reihe Peugeot, Modell »Bébé«, Konstruktion Ettore Bugatti: 1911, 1913, 1912, 1915 (4 cyl., 55 x 90 mm, 850 cc., 10 hp/2000). Links das Fahrgestell eines Bébé 1913.

En haut, une série de «Bébé» Peugeot, construites par Ettore Bugatti: 1911, 1913, 1912, 1915 (4 cyl., 55 x 90 mm, 850 cc., 10 hp/2000). À gauche le châssis d'une Bébé de 1913.

Above, a row of Bébé Peugeots, designed by Ettore Bugatti: 1911, 1913, 1912, 1915 (4 cyl., 55 x 90 mm, 850 cc., 12 hp/2000). At left, the chassis of a 1913 Bébé.

Links/à gauche/left:
Peugeot Type 172 Quadrilette 1922 (4 cyl., 50 x 80 mm, 667 cc., 9.5 hp/2000).

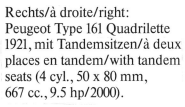

Rechts/à droite/right:
Peugeot Type 161 Quadrilette 1921, mit Tandemsitzen/à deux places en tandem/with tandem seats (4 cyl., 50 x 80 mm, 667 cc., 9.5 hp/2000).

Rechts/à droite/right:
Peugeot SS (sans soupapes)
Type 174/18 CV 1927 (4 cyl.,
95 x 135 mm, 3828 cc., 75 hp/
3500).

Links/à gauche/left:
Peugeot SS Type 174/18 CV
Coach 1927.

Unten/ci-dessous/below:
Porsche 908 Langheck 1969
(8 cyl., 85 x 66 mm, 2997 cc.
350 PS/8400; Siffert/Redman:
1000 km Monza 1969; Jöst/
Casoni/Weber: Le Mans 1972).

Rechts/à droite/right:
Renault 3.5 hp 1900 (1 cyl.,
80 x 80 mm, 402 cc., de Dion).

Oben/ci-dessus/above:
Renault 10 hp Double Phaeton
1903 (2 cyl., 100 x 120 mm,
1884 cc.).

Unten/ci-dessous/below:
Renault AG 1 Double Phaeton
1907 (2 cyl., 80 x 120 mm,
1205 cc.).

Oben/ci-dessus/above:
Renault AX 1908
(2 cyl., 80 x 100 mm, 1205 cc.).

Unten/ci-dessous/below:
Renault Type C Tonneau 1900
(1 cyl., 50 x 90 mm, 450 cc.,
4.5 hp, Aster).

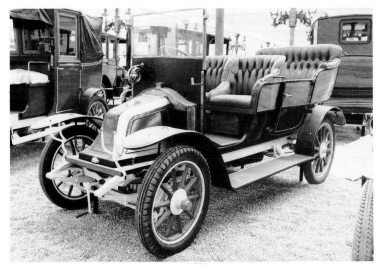

Links/à gauche/left:
Renault AG 1 «Taxi de la
Marne» 1908 (2 cyl., 80 x
120 mm, 1205 cc.).

Unten/ci-dessous/below:
Renault AX 1911 (mit jünge-
rem Markenzeichen/avec un
écusson plus récent/with later
emblem).

Oben/ci-dessus/above:
Renault AX 1912 (ohne Rei-
fen/sans pneu/without tyres).

Oben/ci-dessus/above:
Renault Type EU 1914 (4 cyl.,
80 x 140 mm, 2812 cc.).

Links/à gauche/left:
Renault AX Phaeton 1913

Oben/en haut/above:
Renault Type NM 40 CV
Sedanca-Landaulet (Kellner,
Paris) 1924 (6 cyl., 110 x
160 mm, 9121 cc.).

Rechts/à droite/right:
Renault EU Double Phaeton
1914 (4 cyl., 80 x 140 mm,
2812 cc.).

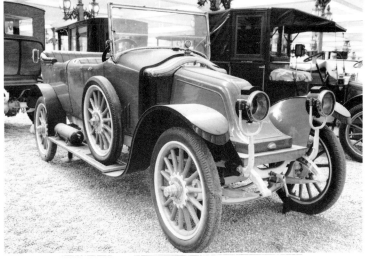

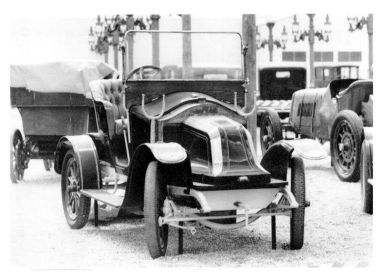

Oben/ci-dessus/above:
Renault AX 1913.

Rechts/à droite/right:
Renault VB 20 CV Limousine
1914 (4 cyl., 100 x 140 mm,
4396 cc.).

Links/à gauche/left:
Ripert-Fahrgestell mit Motor und separate Tonneau-Karosserie, 1901 (2 cyl., 12 hp).

Châssis Ripert et carrosserie tonneau, 1901 (2 cyl., 12 hp).

Ripert chassis frame with engine and separate tonneau body, 1901 (2 cyl., 12 hp).

Rechts/à droite/right:
Rhéda Voiturette 1899 (1 cyl., 2.5 hp).

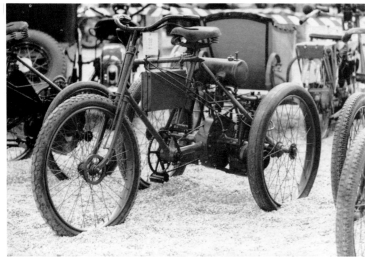

Oben/ci-dessus/above:
Rochet Tricycle 1898 (1 cyl., 4.5 hp Aster).

Rechts/à droite/right:
Ravel 12 CV Limousine 1927 (4 cyl., 2110 cc.).

Rochet-Schneider RS Phaeton
1912 (4 cyl.).

Rechts/à droite/right:
Rochet-Schneider 18 CV Torpédo 1924 (4 cyl.).

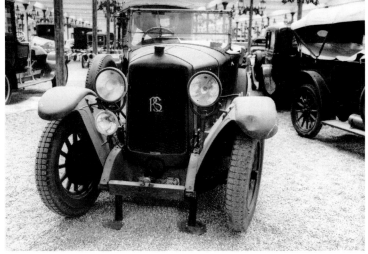

Links/à gauche/left:
Sage 24 hp 1906 (4 cyl.).

Oben/en haut/
above:
Rolls-Royce Silver
Ghost 1912 (6 cyl.,
114 x 120 mm,
7410 cc., 65 hp/1750);
Chassis no. 2076 E.

Links/à gauche/left:
Rolls-Royce 20 hp
Saloon 1922 (6 cyl.,
76 x 114 mm, 3128 cc.,
50 hp/3000).

Oben/ci-dessus/above:
Rolls-Royce Silver Ghost
Cabriolet (Barker) 1921 (6 cyl.,
114 x 120 mm, 7410 cc.).

Rechts/à droite/right:
Rolls-Royce Phantom II
Limousine 1930 (6 cyl., 108 x
140 mm., 7668 cc.).

Rechts/à droite/right:
Rolls-Royce Silver Ghost
Chassis 1922.

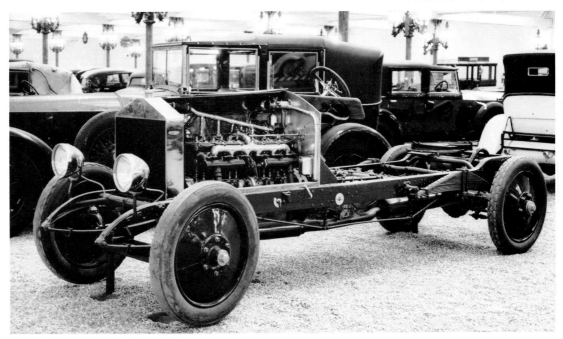

Links/à gauche/left:
Rolls-Royce 25/30 hp Chassis
1936/37 (6 cyl., 89 x 114 mm,
4257 cc.).

Rechts/à droite/right:
Rolls-Royce Silver Ghost
Cabriolet (Barker) 1925 (6 cyl.,
114 x 120 mm, 7410 cc.). Eines
der letzten Modelle mit Vor-
derradbremsen/un des der-
niers modèles avec des freins
sur les roues avant/one of the
last series with front wheel
brakes.

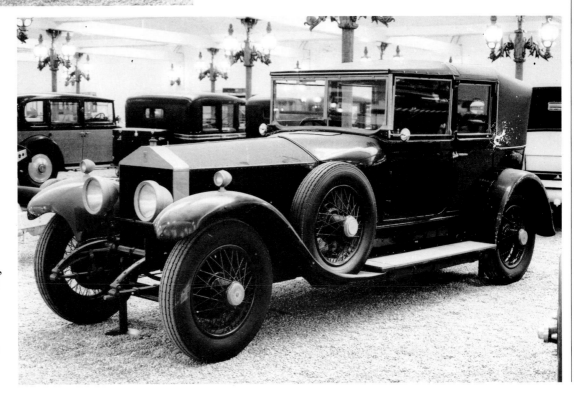

Gegenüberliegende Seite/page
suivante/opposite page:
Rolls-Royce Phantom II 1931,
Rolls-Royce Phantom III
1937 (Freestone & Webb).

Unten/ci-dessous/below:
Rolls-Royce 20 HP Cabriolet
1928 (6 cyl., 76 x 114 mm,
3128 cc.).

Oben/en haut/above:
Rolls-Royce Phantom II
Limousine (Barker) 1933
(6 cyl., 108 x 140 mm, 7668 cc.).

Unten/ci-dessous/below:
Rolls-Royce Phantom III
Limousine (Binder, Paris)
1937 (12 cyl., 82.5 x 114 mm,
7340 cc.).

Oben/en haut/above:
Rolls-Royce Phantom III
Limousine (Hooper) 1938
(12 cyl., 82,5 x 114 mm,
7340 cc.).

Rechts/à droite/right:
Rolls-Royce Phantom III
Limousine (Vandenplas) 1938.

Rechts/à droite/right:
Rolls-Royce Phantom I Sedanca de Ville
1929 (6 cyl., 108 x 140 mm, 7668 cc.).

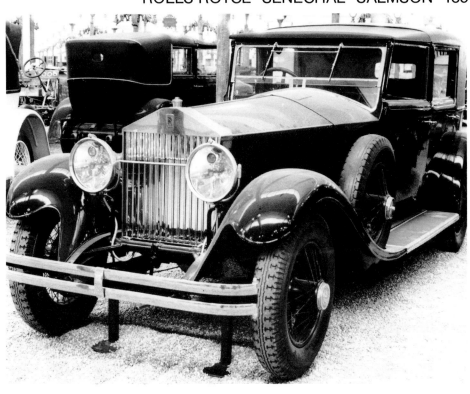

Links/à gauche/left:
Sénéchal Sport Roadster 1923 (4 cyl.,
58 x 95 mm, 1004 cc., Amilcar).

Unten/ci-dessous/below:
Salmson Grand Sport 1926 (4 cyl., 62 x
90 mm, 1086 cc., 2 ohc).

Oben/en haut/above:
Serpollet Dampfwagen/véhi-
cule à vapeur/steam car 1899
(châssis).

Rechts/à droite/right:
Gardner-Serpollet 8 hp
Dampfwagen/véhicule à
vapeur/steam car 1902.

Oben/en haut/above:
Serpollet 40 hp Course (circuit du Nord alcohol) 1902, 4 cyl., Dampfmaschine mit Kardan- antrieb/machine à vapeur 4 cyl., transmission à cardan/4 cyl. steam engine with shaft drive.

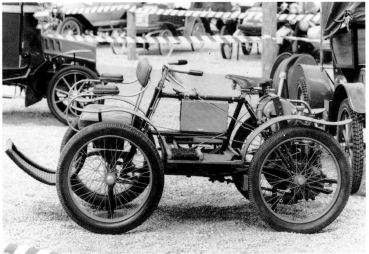

Links/à gauche/left:
Soncin Quadricycle 4.5 hp 1900.

Oben/ci-dessus/above:
Gardner-Serpollet Dampfwagen/véhicule à vapeur/steam car 1900 (4 cyl., 10 hp).

Oben/ci-dessus/above:
Gardner-Serpollet Phaeton Dampfwagen/véhicule à vapeur/steam car 1904 (4 cyl., 18 hp).

Rechts/à droite/right:
Sizaire-Naudin 10 hp Course 1908 (1 cyl., 120 x 110 mm, 1490 cc.), Einzelradaufhängung vorn/roues à suspension indépendante/i.f.s.

Oben/en haut/above:
SS.I 16 hp 1935 (6 cyl., 65,5 x
106 mm, 2143 cc., 53 hp).

Oben/ci-dessus/above:
Steyr 220 Cabriolet 2/4 pl.
(Gläser) 1935 (6 cyl., 73 x
90 mm, 2260 cc., 55 hp/3800).

Rechts/à droite/right:
Tatra Type 87 1937 (V8, 75 x
84 mm, 2958 cc., 2 ohc, 75 hp/
3500).

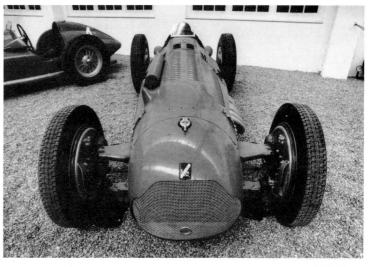

Oben/ci-dessus/above:
Turicum D1 8/18 CV Châssis
1911 (4 cyl., 1940 cc.).

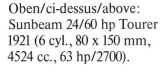

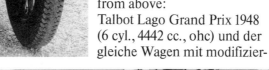

Von oben/de haut en bas/ from above:
Talbot Lago Grand Prix 1948 (6 cyl., 4442 cc., ohc) und der gleiche Wagen mit modifizier- ter Bugpartie/même voiture avec l'avant modifié/same car but with modified radiator grille.

Oben/ci-dessus/above:
Sunbeam 24/60 hp Tourer
1921 (6 cyl., 80 x 150 mm,
4524 cc., 63 hp/2700).

Rechts/à droite/right:
Talbot London 90 1932 (6 cyl.,
69,5 x 100 mm, 2276 cc.,
93 hp/4500).

Links/à gauche/left:
Violet-Bogey Sport 1914 (4 cyl.,
73 x 130 mm, 1088 cc., 22 hp/
2400). Reibrad-Getriebe und
Kettenantrieb/boîte à friction
et transmission par chaîne/
friction drive transmission and
final drive by chain.

Rechts/à droite/right:
Voisin C.18 Diane 1934 (12 cyl.,
72 x 100 mm, 4800 cc., 115 hp).

Oben/ci-dessus/above:
Voisin 13 CV C.11 1927 (6 cyl.,
67 x 110 mm, 2300 cc., 66 hp/
Knight).

Rechts/à droite/right:
Voisin 13 CV C.14 1929 (6 cyl.,
67 x 110 mm, 2300 cc., 66 hp/
Knight).

Links/à gauche/left:
Le Zèbre 6 CV Torpédo 1912
(4 cyl., 50 x 120 mm, 950 cc.).

Unten/ci-dessous/below:
Le Zèbre 4 CV Torpédo 1912
(1 cyl., 85 x 106 mm, 600 cc.).

Rechts/à
droite/right:
Le Zèbre
Torpédo 8 CV
1914 (4 cyl.,
50 x 120 mm,
950 cc.).

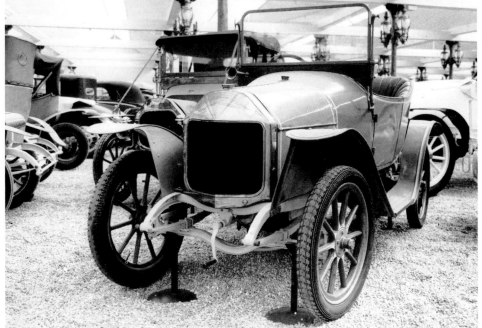

Unten/ci-dessous/below:
Le Zèbre Type A 5 CV
1909 (1 cyl., 58 x 106 mm,
600 cc.).

Links/à gauche/left:
Zwei weitere Le Zèbre 1 Zylinder 1911 und 4 Zylinder
1913/encore deux «Zèbre», 1911 monocylindre et 1913
4 cylindres/two more Le Zèbre, a 1911 single cylinder
and a 1913 4 cylinder model.

Links/à gauche/left:
Zédel (Pontarlier) 9 CV Coupé
Docteur 1911 (4 cyl.).

Oben/ci-dessus/above:
Scott Sociable Dreirad/trois
roues/three-wheeler 1920
(2 cyl., 73 x 63.5 mm, 532 cc.).

Rechts/à droite/right:
Zédel 16 hp Tourer 1912
(4 cyl.).

Links/à gauche/left:
Moto ABC (Gnome & Rhône,
lic. Sopwith) 1921 (2 cyl.,
398 cc.).

Unten/ci-dessous/below:
Harley-Davidson Twin 1916
(2 cyl., 996 cc.).

Oben/ci-dessus/above:
Neracar 1921 (1 cyl., 269 cc.,
Reibradantrieb/transmission à
friction/friction drive).

Rechts/à droite/right:
Harley-Davidson Twin 1940
(2 cyl., 1196 cc.).

Rechts/à droite/right:
Indian Scout Twin 1942 (2 cyl.,
1200 cc.).

Oben/en haut/above: Eselskarren aus Sizilien/
charrette à âne de Sicile/donkey cart from Sicily.

Rechts/à droite/right: Feuerpumpe ca. 1875/
pompe à bras vers 1875/fire brigade hand pump
about 1875.

Rechts unten/à droite ci-dessous/right below:
Zweispännige Feuerlöschpumpe/pompe à incen-
die attelée/fire brigade pump Hartmann, Schmal-
zer & Cie., Malmerspach.

Alte Bauern-
wagen aus
dem Elsaß/
charrettes de
paysan (Al-
sace)/old
Alsatian
farmer carts.

Oben/ci-dessus/above:
Englisches Hochrad mit Vor-
derrad-Bremse, etwa 1882.
Grand bi (Angleterre) équipé
d'un frein avant. Env. 1882.
Penny-farthing or Ordinary
with front wheel brake, about
1882.

Rechts/à droite/right:
Ähnliches Modell wie oben,
ohne Bremse, etwa 1876/
Même modèle que ci-dessus
mais sans frein. Env. 1876/
similar model as above, but
without brake, about 1876.

Links/à gauche/left:
Historischer Postkutschen-Schlitten, 19. Jahrhundert, von der Strecke Neu St. Johann–Wildhaus (Schweiz)/ Traîneau assurant le service de poste au 19e siècle entre Neu St. Johann et Wildhaus en Suisse/ Horse-drawn sledge of the Swiss Mail Neu St. Johann – Wildhaus (19th century).

Unten/ci-dessous/below:
Fahrrad von Micheaux, Paris, mit Rundpedalen, etwa 1867/bicyclette Micheaux à pédales rondes, Paris vers 1867/Micheaux bicycle, Paris, with round-shaped pedals, about 1867.

Rechts/à droite/right:
Fahrrad Vélocipède Lallement (ehemaliger Mitarbeiter Micheaux') etwa 1868/Vélo-cipède Lallement, ancien employé de Micheaux, env. 1868/bicycle Vélocipède Lallement, formerly Micheaux employee, about 1868.

Daneben/à côté/far right:
Ein gleiches Lallement-Fahr-rad/autre vélocipède Lalle-ment/a similar Lallement cycle.

Rechts/à droite/right: Micheaux 1867 wie oben/cf. ci-dessus/ as above.

Französisches Sicherheits-Fahrrad, System Rover, etwa 1889/bicyclette française «de sécurité» système Rover, vers 1889/ French safety bicycle, Rover system, about 1889.

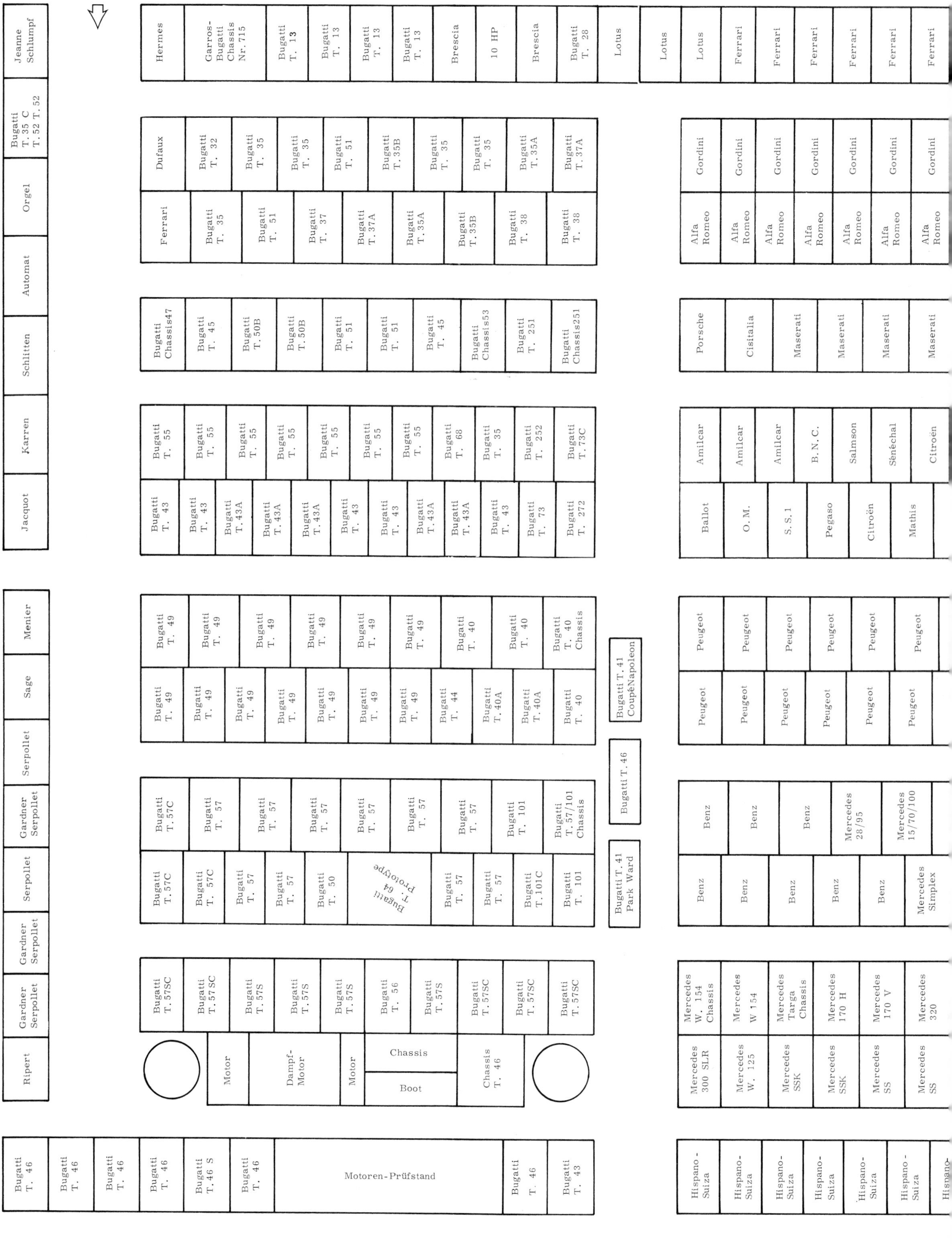

Left vertical column (top to bottom):
- Jeanne Schlumpf
- Bugatti T. 35 C T. 52 T. 52
- Orgel
- Automat
- Schlitten
- Karren
- Jacquot
- Menier
- Sage
- Serpollet
- Gardner Serpollet
- Serpollet
- Gardner Serpollet
- Gardner Serpollet
- Ripert

Row 1: Hermes | Garros-Bugatti Chassis Nr. 715 | Bugatti T. 13 | Bugatti T. 13 | Bugatti T. 13 | Bugatti T. 13 | Brescia | 10 HP | Brescia | Bugatti T. 28 | Lotus | Lotus | Lotus | Ferrari | Ferrari | Ferrari | Ferrari | Ferrari

Row 2: Dufaux | Bugatti T. 32 | Bugatti T. 35 | Bugatti T. 35 | Bugatti T. 51 | Bugatti T. 35B | Bugatti T. 35 | Bugatti T. 35 | Bugatti T. 35A | Bugatti T. 37A | | Gordini | Gordini | Gordini | Gordini | Gordini | Gordini | Gordini

Row 3: Ferrari | Bugatti T. 35 | Bugatti T. 51 | Bugatti T. 37 | Bugatti T. 37A | Bugatti T. 35A | Bugatti T. 35B | Bugatti T. 38 | Bugatti T. 38 | | Alfa Romeo | Alfa Romeo | Alfa Romeo | Alfa Romeo | Alfa Romeo | Alfa Romeo | Alfa Romeo

Row 4: Bugatti Chassis47 | Bugatti T. 45 | Bugatti T. 50B | Bugatti T. 50B | Bugatti T. 51 | Bugatti T. 51 | Bugatti T. 45 | Bugatti Chassis53 | Bugatti T. 251 | Bugatti Chassis251 | | Porsche | Cisitalia | Maserati | Maserati | Maserati | Maserati

Row 5: Bugatti T. 55 | Bugatti T. 55 | Bugatti T. 55 | Bugatti T. 55 | Bugatti T. 55 | Bugatti T. 55 | Bugatti T. 55 | Bugatti T. 68 | Bugatti T. 35 | Bugatti T. 252 | Bugatti T. 73C | | Amilcar | Amilcar | Amilcar | B.N.C. | Salmson | Sénéchal | Citroën

Row 6: Bugatti T. 43 | Bugatti T. 43 | Bugatti T. 43A | Bugatti T. 43A | Bugatti T. 43A | Bugatti T. 43 | Bugatti T. 43 | Bugatti T. 43A | Bugatti T. 43A | Bugatti T. 43 | Bugatti T. 73 | Bugatti T. 272 | | Ballot | O. M. | S. S. 1 | Pegaso | Citroën | Mathis | Citroën

Row 7: Bugatti T. 49 | Bugatti T. 49 | Bugatti T. 49 | Bugatti T. 49 | Bugatti T. 49 | Bugatti T. 49 | Bugatti T. 49 | Bugatti T. 40 | Bugatti T. 40 | Bugatti T. 40 Chassis | Bugatti T. 41 Coupé Napoleon | | Peugeot | Peugeot | Peugeot | Peugeot | Peugeot | Peugeot

Row 8: Bugatti T. 49 | Bugatti T. 49 | Bugatti T. 49 | Bugatti T. 49 | Bugatti T. 49 | Bugatti T. 49 | Bugatti T. 49 | Bugatti T. 44 | Bugatti T. 40A | Bugatti T. 40A | Bugatti T. 40 | Bugatti T. 46 | | Peugeot | Peugeot | Peugeot | Peugeot | Peugeot | Peugeot

Row 9: Bugatti T. 57C | Bugatti T. 57 | Bugatti T. 57 | Bugatti T. 57 | Bugatti T. 57 | Bugatti T. 57 | Bugatti T. 57 | Bugatti T. 101 | Bugatti T. 57/101 Chassis | | Benz | Benz | Benz | Mercedes 28/95 | Mercedes 15/70/100

Row 10: Bugatti T. 57C | Bugatti T. 57C | Bugatti T. 57 | Bugatti T. 57 | Bugatti T. 50 | Bugatti T. 64 Prototype | Bugatti T. 57 | Bugatti T. 57 | Bugatti T. 101C | Bugatti T. 101 | Bugatti T. 41 Park Ward | | Benz | Benz | Benz | Benz | Benz | Mercedes Simplex

Row 11: Bugatti T. 57SC | Bugatti T. 57 SC | Bugatti T. 57S | Bugatti T. 57S | Bugatti T. 57S | Bugatti T. 56 | Bugatti T. 57S | Bugatti T. 57SC | Bugatti T. 57SC | Bugatti T. 57SC | | Mercedes W. 154 Chassis | Mercedes W. 154 | Mercedes Targa Chassis | Mercedes 170 H | Mercedes 170 V | Mercedes 320

Bottom area: Motor | Dampf-Motor | Motor | Chassis / Boot | Chassis T. 46 | | Mercedes 300 SLR | Mercedes W. 125 | Mercedes SSK | Mercedes SSK | Mercedes SS | Mercedes SS

Bottom row (below main): Bugatti T. 46 | Bugatti T. 46 | Bugatti T. 46 | Bugatti T. 46 | Bugatti T. 46 S | Bugatti T. 46 | Motoren-Prüfstand | Bugatti T. 46 | Bugatti T. 43 | | Hispano-Suiza | Hispano-Suiza | Hispano-Suiza | Hispano-Suiza | Hispano-Suiza | Hispano-Suiza | Hispano-Suiza | Hispano-

Ferrari | Ferrari | Talbot | Talbot

Alfa Romeo | Gordini | Simca-Gordini | Simca-Gordini
Gordini | Gordini | Gordini | Gordini

B

Maserati | Maserati | Maserati

Ballot | Citroën | Sunbeam | Tatra | Talbot
Voisin | Voisin | Voisin

Peugeot | Peugeot | Peugeot
Peugeot | Peugeot | Peugeot | Peugeot
Peugeot | Peugeot

Mercedes 380 | Mercedes 300 S | Mercedes 300 S
Mercedes | Mercedes K | Mercedes 630

Chassis | Mercedes 540 K | Mercedes 300 SL | Mercedes 7,7 Chassis
Mercedes 540 K | Mercedes 540 K | Mercedes 7,7

Bugatti T. 50 Chassis | Bugatti T. 46 Chassis | Bugatti T. 46 S Chassis

Fouilleron | Darracq | Darracq | Darracq | Delage | Delage | Barré | Clément | Clément | De Dion | Rochet | De Dion | Scott
Decau ill | Gladiator | Grégoire | Gui | La Licorne | MAF | G. Richard | G. Richard | Indian | Harley | Harley | Moto ABC Neracar

ier | G. Richard | Clément
Hurtu | G. Richard | Clément

Barré | Maurer | Violet | Esculape | Piccolo | Piccolo | Piccolo
Hurtu | Bollée | Monet | Monet | Soncin | Rhéda

Le Zèbre | Le Zèbre | Le Zèbre | Le Zèbre | Fiat Balilla | Fiat | Steyr | Charron | Rochet | Rochet | Mors | Mors
Le Zèbre | Le Zèbre
Turicum | Sizaire-Naudin | Torpedo | Philos | Zédel | Zédel | Ravel | Brasier | Brasier | Darracq | Pic-Pic

Delahaye | Delahaye | De Dion | De Dion | De Dion | De Dion | De Dion | De Dion | De Dion | De Dion | De Dion | De Dion
Delahaye | De Dion
De Dion | De Dion | De Dion | De Dion | De Dion | De Dion | De Dion | De Dion | De Dion | De Dion | De Dion | De Dion

Renault | Renault | Renault | Renault | Renault | Renault | Renault | Renault | Renault | Renault
Renault
Renault | Panhard | Panhard | Panhard | Panhard | Panhard | Panhard | Panhard | Panhard | Panhard

Rolls Silver Ghost | Rolls Silver Ghost | Rolls 20/25 | Rolls 20 | Rolls 20/25 | Rolls P. 2 | Rolls P. 3 | Bentley | Bentley | Daimler
Rolls Silver Ghost | Rolls Silver Ghost | Rolls P. 1 | Rolls P. 2 | Rolls P. 2 | Rolls P. 3 | Rolls P. 3 | Rolls P. 3 | Daimler | Bentley

Farman | Farman Chassis | Farman | Isotta Fraschini | Isotta Fraschini | Isotta Fraschini | Delaunay | Delaunay | Lorraine | Lorraine | Lorraine Dietrich | Lorraine Dietrich | Lorraine Dietrich

Fahrräder - Bicycles

Maybach | Maybach | Maybach | Maybach | Maybach
Maybach | Maybach
Maybach
Audi
Horch
Lancia | Lancia | Horch
Lancia | Minerva | Horch

Daimler | Daimler | Feuerpumpe
Wagen
Minerva | Wagen
Daimler | Daimler | Pumpe

Austro-Daimler

So zweifelhaft die Umstände sind, denen das Schlumpf-Museum seine Existenz verdankt, so anerkennenswert ist aber auch die Liebe und Sorgfalt, mit der seine Initiatoren die Aufgabe, die sie sich gestellt hatten, realisierten. Die Automobilsammlung der Gebrüder Schlumpf und die Vorgänge des Jahres 1977 werden mit Sicherheit zur Legende unter den Freunden historischer Automobile werden.

Pour aussi troubles que soient les circonstances dans lesquelles le musée Schlumpf a vu le jour et a grandi, il n'en demeure pas moins que le soin et l'amour mis par les initiateurs de l'entreprise à réaliser la tâche qu'ils s'étaient fixée sont remarquables. Pour les amateurs de voitures anciennes, la collection automobile des frères Schlumpf et les événements de l'année 1977 passeront certainement dans la légende.

Circumstances, under which the Schlumpf collection was established, can be described as doubtful. However, we have to admire the love and care and good taste with which the collection has been put together. The Mulhouse museum and the 1977 proceedings in the Schlumpf case will become legend.